ABOUT THE AUTHOR

Jenny and le ̲er in finance ̲ɹotessional life with a o̲ɡɩee in Mathematics from the University of Oxford and going on to qualify as an actuary.

Jenny worked in technical actuarial roles and as a pensions and investment consultant before gravitating towards the people side of the business, specialising in leading sales teams for large asset management companies. She now has a portfolio-style career and is a regular speaker on resilience, business communication, hybrid working, motivation and workplace culture.

When she is not working or being entertained by her three fabulous sons, Jenny spends her time preparing for a piano diploma, running half-marathons and taking (what she hopes are) beautiful photographs.

 @j3nsegal   www.jennysegal.co.uk

PREVIOUS PUBLICATIONS

This is the third book in Jenny's series on motivation at work. Here are some of the reviews of Building Better Workplace Cultures (kdp, 2021) and Purpose & Hybrid Working (kdp, 2023):

"The book of our time"
Imran Qureshi – Head of North America, WTW

"What a thought-provoking book! The creative prompts led me to re-evaluate the importance of the workplace as a community and source of happiness"
Sally Bridgeland – Chair, Impax Asset Management Group

"Packed with socially-researched insight, compassion and actionable ideas"
Calum Cooper – Chair of Partnership Council, Hymans Robertson

"Very gripping, thought-provoking, invites you to pause and think"
Paul Price – Founder & CEO, Haven Green

"Helpfully illustrated by case studies and nuanced discussion"
Aoifinn Devitt – Chief Investment Officer, Moneta

"Our firm works with financial organizations around the world, and all of them have asked for advice about hybrid work. Jenny's book provides the answers. Well written, fun to read, and powerfully informative. Highly recommended"
Jim Ware, CFA – Founder, Focus Consulting Group
Author of six books on leadership and culture

"Combining innovative new thinking and content without losing the insights of its survey cohort, this book delivers hybrid working's best practices in a really enjoyable read"
Hugh Cutler – Global Distribution Leader

"Stimulates new ideas and concepts that we can all grasp and start working with straight away"
Michelle Elstein - Founder, Courageous Co.

"Brilliantly engaging and insightful call to rethink how we work"
Annabel Gillard – Organisational Culture & Ethics Expert

On Motivation:

Board Effectiveness & Culture

Jenny Segal

ISBN 979-8-8644-8010-6

For my fabulous friends

In Perfect Balance

PREFACE

Following in the footsteps of its predecessor volumes **On Motivation: Building Better Workplace Cultures** and **On Motivation: Purpose & Hybrid Working**, this synthesis of the views of a host of practitioners is presented in what, I hope, is an informative, crisp and entertaining style.

Peppered with quotes, case studies, photographs and cultural references, I have adopted a colour-coded system for ease of reference:

> *"Quotes from my reference group are in blue"*

Case Studies

are in green

LEARNING POINTS

are in lilac

- and are credited here

CHAPTER SUMMARIES

1. are in

2. purple

I hope you enjoy reading it. But most of all I hope that its learnings will help you to build better, more effective boards which drive happier, more impactful outcomes for the stakeholders they serve.

WITH THANKS TO...

This research is an amalgamation of the wisdom, experience and thoughtfulness of its contributors: I am exceptionally grateful to them for both their time and their openness. To ensure the latter, I have not listed them by name.

And a huge thank-you to friend and mentor **Sally Bridgeland** for hatching this project with me and to **Korn Ferry, The McLean Partnership, Tyzack Partners, Avida International** and **Hansuke** for their support.

CONTENTS

TABLE OF PHOTOGRAPHS.. xii

TABLE OF FIGURES xiii

1. **INTRODUCTION** 17

2. **THE RESEARCH** 19

   2.1 PARTICIPANTS 19
   2.2 THE QUESTIONNAIRE 21

3. **BOARD EFFECTIVENESS** 24

   3.1 SUMMARY 24
   3.2 MEASURING EFFECTIVENESS.................................... 25
   3.3 THE GOOD 28
   3.4 THE BAD 32
   3.5 THE UGLY 35

4. **CHAIRING** 40

   4.1 SUMMARY 40
   4.2 THE CONDUCTOR... 41
   4.3 WHAT GOOD LOOKS LIKE 41
   4.4 EFFECTIVE CHAIRING.. 43
   4.5 THE CHAIRING CYCLE 44
   4.6 WHAT'S ON THE AGENDA?... 49

5. **BOARD COMPOSITION** 53

   5.1 SUMMARY 53
   5.2 CULTURE 55
   5.3 CHEMISTRY.. 56
   5.4 BOARD DINNERS ET AL 61
   5.5 TRAINING 65
   5.6 HIRING 67
   5.7 SKILLS V STRENGTHS 71
   5.8 DIVERSITY 74
   5.9 SMALL IS BEAUTIFUL 82
   5.10 IN THE MIX... 86

6. BOARD PAPERS **91**

    6.1 SUMMARY 91
    6.2 BOARD PORTALS 92
    6.3 THE THOUSAND PAGE BOARD PACK 94
    6.4 THE PERFECT PAPER 97
    6.5 DON'T BE LATE 102

7. BOARD MEETINGS **104**

    7.1 SUMMARY 104
    7.2 TO ZOOM OR NOT TO ZOOM? 105
    7.3 TECHSTRACTION 111
    7.4 OILING THE WHEELS 114

8. OTHER THOUGHTS **122**

    8.1 SUMMARY 122
    8.2 EMPLOYEE ENGAGEMENT 123
    8.3 OVER-BOARDING 124
    8.4 DIRECTORS' REMUNERATION 125
    8.5 SECURING THAT ELUSIVE FIRST NED 126

9. IN CONCLUSION **129**

INDEX **131**

TABLE OF PHOTOGRAPHS

In Perfect Balance v

Mystical Colour 16

Coffee Break 18

See The Light 23

Into The Light... 39

A Riot of Colours.. 52

Jam Before Cream or Cream Before Jam? 74

Chess Club - Drama Club 79

The Beverage You Are About To Enjoy Is Extremely Hot 90

Peeling Back The Layers.. 97

Ernest Hemingway.. 100

City Buzz 103

Time Waits For No Man... 119

Hidden Secrets 121

Rainbow Connection 128

Brave and Beautiful 130

Stairway To Wisdom 133

TABLE OF FIGURES

Survey Participants By Gender 19

Survey Participants By Age 20

Survey Participants by Years of Board Experience......................... 20

The Effectiveness Barometer... 26

The Effectiveness Barometer Spread.. 27

Board Effectiveness Drivers 28

The Effective Chair.. 42

The Chairing Cycle 44

Bad Cultures 55

Board Dinners Are Highly Valued 61

Typical Board Skills Matrix.. 72

Optimal Board Size 89

How To Structure A Fantastic Board Paper..................................... 98

Board

Effectiveness

&

Culture

Mystical Colour

1. INTRODUCTION

board *noun [usually singular]*:

the group of people who are responsible for controlling and organising a company or organisation

– Cambridge Dictionary

"There is a danger that we overly complicate thinking or aggrandise being on a board. It's simply a role for experienced individuals who want to do the job. A board meeting should be like any other meeting. Don't make it into a torture chamber if you want to get the best out of your people"

Dramatised in 'Succession[1]', parodied by Monty Python[2] and 'The Fall and Rise of Reginald Perrin[3]', hallowed in Lord Alan Sugar's 'The Apprentice', the boardroom is a mystical cauldron in which the fortunes of companies and the futures of their employees are decreed. Its secret goings-on determine whether we have jobs and drive the success of our economies.

The board director carries a weighty responsibility for strategy, control and advice. What is done well, what can be done better and what can board directors learn from each other to improve their own and their boards' effectiveness?

To answer these questions, during the summer of 2023 I interviewed a group of Non-Executive Directors ('NEDs') to find out their thoughts on board culture and effectiveness.

---

[1] Jesse Armstrong, 2018
[2] 'The Crimson Permanent Assurance' - Terry Gilliam, 1983
[3] 'The Boardroom' - David Hobbs, 1976

Coffee Break

2. THE RESEARCH

2.1 PARTICIPANTS

I recruited 47 participants - the Board Effectiveness & Culture 2023 Reference Group (my 'reference group') - from a combination of my own network, a LinkedIn request and introductions from search firms Korn Ferry and The McLean Partnership. All participants bar one were in the Financial Services sector, sitting on a collective **189 boards, chairing 61** of them and with combined experience of **634 years**. The majority were UK-based.

Participants were assured anonymity to ensure they could express their views freely. However, the graphs below provide some insights into their demographics.

Split roughly **50:50 by gender**, participants had a **median age of 60.5**, males being on average older (62.5) than females (58.0)

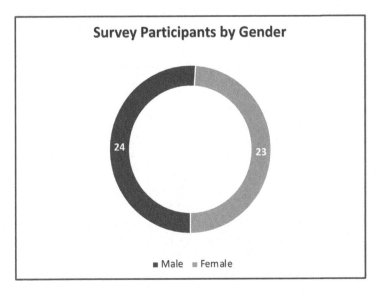

Figure 2.1 – Survey Participants By Gender

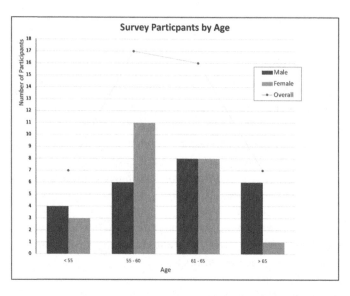

Figure 2.2 – Survey Participants By Age

with **15.0 years' median board experience,** males being marginally less experienced (13.5 years) than females (15.0 years).

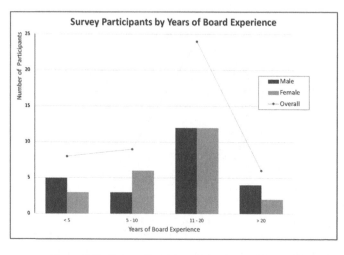

Figure 2.3 - Survey Participants by Years of Board Experience

2.2 THE QUESTIONNAIRE

These were the questions I asked my reference group:

DEMOGRAPHICS

- What is your age and your gender?
- How long have you been a board member?
- How many boards do you sit on?
- How many do you chair?

BOARD EFFECTIVENESS

On a scale of 1 to 10, where

1 is ineffective and
10 is outstandingly effective

what score would you assign to the most and least effective boards you have worked with over your career?

Why have you arrived at that score?

MEETING MECHANICS

- What are your thoughts on:
- in-person v 100% virtual v hybrid meetings
- the importance of board dinners
- IT
- the quality of board papers?

What tips do you have for effective chairing?

BOARD COMPOSITION

What are your views on the optimal board size?

What is the right mix of NEDs to Execs?

What are your thoughts on board chemistry and how we should think about:

- hiring
- skills v strengths/qualities
- diversity?

FINAL THOUGHTS

What other boardroom advice and wisdom can you share?

See The Light

3. BOARD EFFECTIVENESS

3.1 SUMMARY

1. Self-reflection can improve board effectiveness. This encompasses regular Effectiveness Reviews, where the findings are incorporated into actions, and having reflection time as a standing agenda item

2. Having an outstanding chair is the key driver of an effective board

3. The quality of individual board members is very important, but there also needs to be the right mix of skills and diversity of thought

4. An effective board has a clearly defined and well-understood purpose

5. Board papers need to be clear and timely. Investing in a fit-for-purpose company secretariat function may be money well-spent

6. Respect is paramount. This aids board chemistry and helps to establish a good exec/non-exec dynamic which is an important determinant of effectiveness

3.2 MEASURING EFFECTIVENESS

Appointing the chief executive, overseeing the running of the business, providing strategic guidance and wisdom, the board has a crucial role in driving the success of a company. Some excel at it, whilst others fail. No board director wants to waste their time and skills sitting on an ineffective, incompetent board; how can we measure, and improve, their effectiveness?

EFFECTIVENESS REVIEWS

Many boards hold regular effectiveness reviews, sometimes driven by regulatory requirement but often by choice, reflecting a desire for self-improvement. These take a variety of formats: 360 director appraisals, informal annual reviews, and very formal triennial audits conducted by an external provider.

Interpreted wisely, this feedback can be a good way to measure and improve the board and to weave a consistent golden thread through the business.

> *"We hold really good evaluation sessions once a year and we go on to incorporate many of the suggestions into our practices. These have included our team and meeting dynamics and how to organise agendas - very pedestrian, but it makes a huge difference. We have introduced new dimensions to the way we operate, now visiting service centres and including 'white space' at the start or end of the meeting to allow time for reflection"*

However, effectiveness reviews can sometimes be overly focused on what is easy to measure, rather than the more mercurial, subjective aspects such as preparedness, willingness to speak up in meetings and a blue-sky assessment of what might be missing.

THE EFFECTIVENESS BAROMETER

To get underneath this, I sought a quantitative, albeit subjective, measure of board effectiveness, asking my reference group to rate on a scale of 1 to 10 the most and least effective boards they had experienced over their entire board careers. My findings are shown in the charts below:

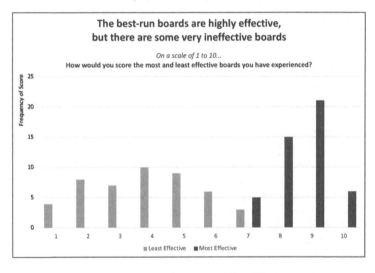

Figure 3.1 - The Effectiveness Barometer

The most effective boards scored highly, between 7 and 10: when boards are effective, they are often *really* effective. But even the best boards have room for improvement.

The least effective boards ranged from 1 to 7, with a fair number scoring very poorly indeed.

> *"When all noses point in the same direction and the strategy*
> *is agreed, not second-guessed, it easily gets up to a 7.*
> *But when there is disagreement on strategy, it descends*
> *into a free-for-all, driven by individuals' hobby horses"*

For each pair of scores, I then looked at the difference and plotted the spread as the dotted purple line below. It peaks twice at 4 and 6, illustrating that a significant number of my reference group have experienced the good, the bad and the ugly in their board careers.

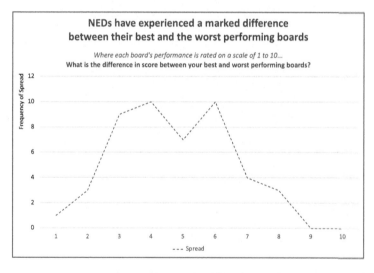

Figure 3.2 - The Effectiveness Barometer Spread

I then dug into the reasons behind the scores.

3.3 THE GOOD

Across my reference group, there was a high degree of consensus about what makes a great board.

Figure 3.3 - Board Effectiveness Drivers
Copyright © 2023 Jenny Segal

"It's all about the chair"

An **outstanding chair** was universally considered to be the most important driver of board effectiveness.

> *"We had a fantastic, amazing chair. They had an open style, involved everyone and were fair and decisive. The organisation was completely open to working with the board"*

Case Study: The Inexperienced Chair

The best board I sat on had a very good blend of skills, coupled with great alignment and purpose. Diversity can lead to misalignment, but having a clearly-defined, common goal counters this. It was helped by very thoughtful chairing from a low ego, highly accomplished businessman who was not an established chair. Knowing he needed to bring out the best in the board, he spent a lot of time thinking about how to draw on our experience. This led to good hiring, clear Exec/NED delineation and feedback on goals and aspirations, delivered in an actionable format.

The reference group prized a **diverse** group of **skilled** individuals, operating with a clear purpose, informed by **timely, well-written board papers.**

> *"As a board, we had a lot to deal with, including the unexpected death of the CEO and then having to let down lots of succession candidates gently. It really helped us to bond as a group"*

A **strong company secretariat function** can make all the difference, ensuring that papers are on-point, concise and consistent, that the board is proactively informed of issues, upcoming regulation etc ahead of time and that meetings are diarised well in advance, avoiding last-minute changes. Minimising the administrative noise allows the board to focus on the right things and promotes more challenging and deeper discussions.

> *"Having great committee chairs is essential. It makes the board so much more effective and gives space to focus on strategy"*

A healthy **dynamic between the exec and the non-exec** featured heavily, enabling the board to add real value to the executive thinking.

Respect is key to building good board chemistry, allowing difficult conversations to be constructive rather than adversarial or career-defining. It also helps in establishing a healthy **exec/non-exec dynamic**, unlocking access to the broader executive and senior leadership teams and thus leading to a sophisticated understanding of the organisation.

> **Case Study: A Young Business**
>
> I work with a very young company with a very diverse, small board. Everyone is well-aligned with the company's mission, shares information ahead of time and gives feedback on the materials. Meetings are always intentional, with a laser-sharp focus on the key areas which people are well-prepared to discuss.

The best-performing boards are self-aware and **seek continuous improvement** via self-reflection, 360 feedback from the chair, fellow directors and the Exec. They have clear objectives: *'Be crisper in your comments on X'*, *'Express your views more on Y'* to which they are held to account, both as a board and as individuals.

FULL MARKS

> **Case Study: 10/10 for Effectiveness**
>
> The Chair's style was really effective. He allowed sufficient time for deep debate, drawing everyone in. The SID[4] had a proper interface role between the board and the chair, and the chair and the CEO had a good programme of engagement with critical shareholders, with no no-go areas. The directors were encouraged to walk the floors and management was not threatened by this. There were effective sub-committees whose chairs were adept at summarising outcomes and decisions. Management information was of the right quality and quantity, with enough time for reading, discussion and side-discussion.

---

[4] Senior Independent Director: Recommended by the 2003 Higgs Review for publicly-listed companies to serve as a sounding board for the chair and to act as an intermediary for other directors.

> *"To get a 10, you need an outstanding chair and the right board composition, so that across the board someone is knowledgeable about everything relevant to the business. There needs to be clarity on how much risk the organisation is willing to take and this should be driven by the Board, not the execs"*

3.4 THE BAD

> *"Some boards have a 'Don't rock the boat' culture. The most effective NEDs don't accept the status quo: they challenge"*

Some boards have an **over-dominant chair**, who doesn't elicit views; every idea has to be theirs to be taken forward. Often they will only recruit people in the same mould, leading to groupthink and clubbiness. Others have **weak chairs**, leading to troubled relationships with the CEO and a confusion between the **exec and non-exec authorities**.

> *"It can be very difficult to tell a founder that they need a chief exec"*

> *"It's too easy for it to become 'The CEO Show'"*

Ineffective meetings are a big bug-bear. Some have no agenda, are too long, lack focus or are set up at very short notice, with papers that are poor quality and are delivered too late to be read, or arrive in dribs and drabs. Without a clear steer from the exec, NEDs can be left to read the runes. Often these problems stem from a non-existent or **inadequate company secretariat function**.

> *"A little knowledge and a lack of respect of process can open up a random, unnecessary path"*

Others suffer from a **lack of clarity of purpose**. Meetings are unproductive, with huge amounts of time wasted in the weeds of the detail and word-smithing documents. Some descend into box-ticking exercises where all the decisions that matter are taken outside the room.

Case Study: Subsidiary v Parent

The company was a regulated entity and was a UK subsidiary of a US bank. The US do governance differently and there was a general vibe from the parent that what the UK regulator was requiring was over the top. In the first 18 months, the board met 28 times. Engagement from the NEDs was seen as interference in the broader business, so the board quickly descended into a box-ticking exercise to keep the regulator happy, with all the real conversations happening outside the room.

A **lack of honesty and transparency** causes many problems, including unspoken disagreement about the direction of travel of the company, and no public debate to air the issues and find a solution.

"People want to hold onto their jobs.
There is still an ability for people to hide and collect their fee"

Dysfunctional boards were a common complaint, plagued with difficult people and personality clashes, impacting decision-making. Challenging behaviours include grandstanding and defensiveness, with an unwillingness to acknowledge lack of industry experience. Another issue is blurring the boundary between the executive and the non-executive functions.

> *"NEDs are not tough enough. You need to be firm and decisive, but not overbearing in your debate with the exec. It's a fine line. If you don't do it with enough vigour, you don't hold their feet to the fire. But too much and you demoralise and demotivate, when you need to support and encourage"*

> *"When CEOs are being fired and decisions are being made in the background as side-deals, NEDs become defensive about their reputations, rather than focusing on the company"*

Boards can just be **too large** to get anything done. **Poor communication** results in some members being well-briefed whilst others know nothing about a topic, wasting valuable time on establishing uniform minimum knowledge levels.

Case Study: Equal votes for non-experts

I am an advocate of member-nominated trustees because they care about the scheme much more than professional trustees. However, on some boards there is no minimum threshold of competence. Yet boards want joint decisions because the directors are jointly responsible, so everyone's vote has to count equally.

On this particular board, there were eight equally-voiced directors, but two were of questionable competence. Decision-making was hard as they were swept along and had to trust their 'expert' colleagues. There was a real danger from a few directors whose confidence outweighed their expertise, as they could sweep along the non-experts with their high degree of conviction. Humility and self-knowledge are really important and they were lacking here.

3.5 THE UGLY

A few boards were scored 1s and 2s for their effectiveness with reasons and examples given below:

POOR CHAIRING

> *"The chair dominated all the discussion. So no one bothered preparing and it was a total waste of time being there"*

> *"The chair was scared of the extremely dominant CEO and wasn't comfortable challenging him. It was hugely difficult for both the CEO and the chair"*

Case Study: Chair in thrall of the CEO

I once served on a board that I would score a '2'. The chair was not independent of the CEO, in fact he was completely in his thrall. He had served for 12 years, and just announced he would stay on for another three - he didn't understand the corporate governance code. There was insufficient rigour. The individuals were weak: a combination of negligence and lack of competence. They didn't understand, they didn't read papers, they didn't respond to emails. And the CEO would get aggressive so that people would shut up.

I didn't give it a '1' because the CEO was competent at running the business".

Case Study: CEO-Board Dysfunction

The CEO didn't know how to use the board. He was scared of it and he became defensive and disengaged. While this happened, both the board and the organisation suffered: performance drifted, the senior leadership team became dispirited and demotivated, and the NEDs disengaged. That continued for a while until the board and a material stakeholder acted together to oust the CEO.

FAILURE TO DELIVER

Case Study: Public board failure

Through dysfunctional board decisions, a restructuring proposition failed to be accepted by this insurance company's members, wasting a lot of time and money.

The blame was spread widely amongst the directors who were too much in the weeds.

The chair had served credibly on other boards but proposed himself as chair of the successor company. There was probably some hubris about this, meaning he was less able to beat off criticism from the press.

Part of the failure arose from the board being too weak in its dealings with the regulator. In doing so, it gained a reputation for erratic behaviour as it was first perceived as mean and then unfairly generous to policyholders.

> *"Something was agreed at Board level and the opposite was done. It was a spectacular governance fail"*

UNMANAGED CONFLICTS OF INTEREST

> *"This was a stakeholder board and people failed to take off their day-job hats at the door. It was all about vested interests. Conflicts were not properly surfaced - they were papered over and couldn't be resolved"*

DOMINANT SHAREHOLDER

Case Study: Dominant shareholder

I was on a board where 40% of the company was owned by one family. The CEO was not a family member and he was fantastic. He managed the relationship with them really well (and it takes a very strong CEO to navigate that pressure) but in reality the chair ran the business from afar. In some ways, it was a cushy life as a non-exec, but that's because there was nothing to do. I would not recommend joining a board with a dominant shareholder.

Case Study: Ticking the box

The company had one or two owners who appointed the majority of the directors. There were very few independent directors, and they were just there to fill the governance gap. Our opinion was not heard. The board didn't have a real governance function, only on paper. We ended up being an approval stamp for decisions that had already been made. It was intensely frustrating to all the independent NEDs and dangerous for our personal brands.

"There was just no shared sense of endeavour. The chair was not interested in addressing the issues; no one was tackling the poorly-performing CEO. It was just bobbing along and nothing was happening"

"The exec and the non-exec were not pointing in the same direction. The chair was sitting in the middle of two arguing parties. Both sides had given up hope"

Into The Light

Copyright © 2023 Jenny Segal

4. CHAIRING

4.1 SUMMARY

1. A great chair is a skilled conductor, bringing in the various moving parts at the right time and weaving them together to produce a coherent, well-orchestrated outcome

2. Chairing skills include humility, reading the room and listening before opining: speaking first is the number one cardinal sin

3. Detailed preparation is necessary to understand what needs to be discussed and reflecting this in a well-structured agenda. Spending time with the exec beforehand ensures the right papers are produced and sufficient time is allocated to discuss them

4. The chair should build trusted rapport with the board members to understand their knowledge, experience and preferred style so as to bring them into the discussion at the right point to deliver maximum value

4.2 THE CONDUCTOR

> **The Conductor**
>
> In an orchestra, the conductor is the outside ear for the group. When you have more than, say, 12 people playing, it becomes increasingly difficult to hear yourself objectively, to follow all the threads. Each individual only contributes a small part toward the whole and the conductor has to have a vision of this whole and direct, drive and inspire the group towards their vision.
>
> You also have to be a skilful manager, a people person, somebody with extraordinary managerial talent. Sometimes it's about getting a fantastic ensemble together, the right blend of professionals, keeping the mystique, being the face of the orchestra. Conductors get paid 100 times more than any orchestral player, yet often we don't even know why they are there. It's a bit of a shamanic job.
>
> **– JM**

The chair is the conductor of the board meeting. They know who to bring in where. Which parts should be loud. And which should be quiet.

4.3 WHAT GOOD LOOKS LIKE

Setting the cultural tone for the board and the company, the chair plays a vitally important role.

I asked my reference group to describe the qualities of an effective chair:

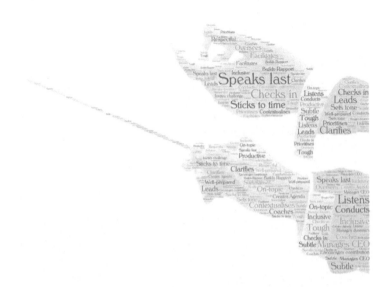

The number one prized behaviour of a good chair is that they solicit opinion first and **they speak last**.

> *"The chair has a greatly under-estimated responsibility.*
> *They determine the effectiveness of the board.*
> *You have a group of people with no previous experience of*
> *each other, all thrown together, all distracted by their busy*
> *lives. It is the chair's role to pull this disparate group together"*

Case Study: The Breathtakingly-Effective Chair

I served on a board which had an incredible chair who employed some simple, but highly effective, techniques:

1. He has a fundamental understanding that **the chair speaks last**. He would draw comments out of other directors with penetrating questions and sublimated his own views until the debate had run its course

2. He insisted that we **sit at a round table**. This has a profound impact on the dynamics: with no head-of-the-table, everyone's view is equally weighted

On points of contention, he would **call on everyone** and get eye contact. This gave the introverts and the conflict-avoidants licence to talk.

"I had one chair who was incredibly bright, but he was bloody lazy and arrogant. He would watch the cricket on his phone during meetings; he could multi-task and be effective, but he didn't realise how rude and demotivating it was.

There was a loquacious and nervous HR director and he would mime slitting his throat to get her to shut up"

4.5 THE CHAIRING CYCLE

Figure 4.2 - The Chairing Cycle

CREATING THE AGENDA

"Getting the agenda timings wrong is the biggest crime. It's like sitting an exam and leaving 10 minutes for the 20-marker"

"I find it frustrating to hear new stuff from the execs in the meeting. It should all be in the papers"

The chair decides which items do and don't need discussing, setting a high bar and flushing out the detail beforehand. The more time spent fine tuning, the better. Once drafted, it should be shared well in advance with the proposed time allocations. It is critical to allow enough time to deep dive into the important and urgent discussions and canvassing the board's opinion helps to get it right.

> *"Trail something. If the board paper is scheduled for September, prime them in March"*

Boards do not necessarily get just one shot at addressing a problem, and nor should they. If a topic is particularly thorny, it may be worth revisiting it before a decision is made.

PREPARING FOR THE MEETING

Good pre-work makes for a better meeting, yet some chairs are not fully-prepared.

> *"The chair should read ALL the papers. Twice"*

> *"As chair, I need to decide what I think the outcome and action will be for everything before the meeting. 70% of the time the outcome is as I expected. It only changes if another NED takes a really strong position"*

Speaking to the CEO and other execs ahead of the meeting is key. It ensures both sides know what to expect, and can circumvent the exec slipping something unexpected onto the agenda. It also provides a forum for mentoring and brainstorming the best way to air particular issues.

> *"Know which parts are contentious with the exec: is it rubber-stamping or is it a fistfight? You don't want the latter in the boardroom"*

The CEO should read all the papers and check that they are representative of business.

It is often valuable for the chair to spend time with the executive team's direct reports. Hearing the issues first hand gives a better sense of what's going on, although this needs to be done with sensitivity so that the exec does not feel threatened.

MANAGING THE TEAM

Chairs have to be tough. A weighty responsibility is to hire and fire the CEO, so they need to make thoughtful and sometimes difficult people decisions. This includes acting quickly to stamp out undesirable behaviour on the board and to imprint the culture they want for their team.

> *"Is the right CEO in place? If 'Yes', support them. If 'No', replace them"*

> *"If individuals are not pulling their weight, if they are idle or unable to contribute, the chair needs to deal with it sooner rather than later. They should get disruptive people off the board as fast as possible "*

Case Study: Pro Bono Boards

It can be hard for chairs to stand their ground with pro bono boards. You get a lot of free-riders, people who want it on their CV, sometimes The Great & The Good. But they don't do much work because they're not getting paid. Their attendance rate is lower than paid board roles and they are often not well prepared.

Chairs should spend meaningful one-on-one time with each director outside the boardroom to build rapport and trust, and to understand their strengths and areas for development, their interests and what motivates them.

> *"Be very purposeful. Think about what you want from each board member and get their input in real time. They should be your most loyal, invested, aligned constituent"*

> *"A lot of NEDs reflect back on their previous experiences, but sometimes things have moved on, so there is a need to contextualise. It is the job of the chair to bring out the relevant aspects in the right way"*

CONDUCTING THE MEETING

Board meetings should contain no surprises. The chair orchestrates the meeting from beginning to end, aiming for a fine balance between obsessively sticking to time and keeping on point, whilst allowing the pertinent issues to be fully aired.

> *"The chair should never allow presenters to go through their papers in detail as it just encourages poor prep. But you do need a bit of framing to tease out interest and to promote an engaged discussion and elicit the appropriate input"*

> *"Remind the presenters that everyone has read the papers. Set the board culture so that everyone **has** read the papers!"*

The chair should **open up the discussion and then be quiet**, eliciting views from all board members before expressing their own.

> *"One chair was a bit of a maverick. He would state an opinion he does not believe in to avoid 'yes' men"*

The chair sets the tone by creating a respectful environment which encourages people to speak up, nipping bad practice in the bud.

"The chair's job is to make sure everyone contributes. To ensure the overbearing mansplainer doesn't take up 90% of the airtime"

Having spent time with each board director prior to the meeting, the chair will know which points each member wants to discuss and where their expertise will bring particular richness to the debate. This can avoid the 'creeping death' of going one-by-one round the boardroom table after each agenda item, asking if anyone has anything else to add. Listening carefully, they should clarify, reflect back, summarise, draw conclusions and tee-up actions from the debate.

It can be helpful to include a 10-to-15-minute slot at the end of the meeting to reflect on how it went: was everyone well-briefed, were the papers good, were the time allocations right, was the discussion strategic, which sessions worked well. This real-time feedback can be healthy and create a culture of openness.

After the meeting, the chair should check in with each member one-on-one to ensure they felt the issues were dealt with. And with the exec team: that they felt valued and supported for their detailed work in preparing papers.

"Chairing is like parenting. You don't need to agree with your children, but they do need to feel heard"

INTRA MEETING

Communicating in the background intra-meeting is powerful. Off-cycle meetings with the execs provide continuous context on the development of the business, which the chair can then pass on to the board.

4.6 WHAT'S ON THE AGENDA?

> *"The chair needs to manage the agenda. It's an important part of the job. It's not just reading the papers and showing up"*

Structuring the agenda well can make all the difference. Board meetings are often long - from a few hours to a few days - so the order in which items are addressed and the length of time allocated to each is worth getting right.

Dealing with topics in the wrong order impedes the flow of decision-making. It does not allow sufficient time, which may result in more esoteric points being overlooked. In addition, the order in which items are tabled determines the concentration and energy levels available for clarity of thought.

Some chairs prefer to deal with the challenging stuff earlier on whilst everyone is still fresh; others prefer to canter through the routine standing items and allocate long chunks to one or two deep dives.

> *"There has been a monumental increase in risk management in financial services. You need to make sure that regulation and compliance don't drown out operations and investment. We deliberately split our time a third, a third, a third"*

Case Study: A Structured Agenda

We found that three-quarters of the agenda was purely operational and backwards-looking and we should generally be agreeing with management. This part has to run efficiently with the right materials. So we decided to structure our board agendas into three distinct parts:

1. Past - legals, financials

2. Present - headwinds

3. Future - strategy

REFLECTION TIME

Scheduling regular self-reflection time into each agenda can raise board effectiveness. This time can be used to be honest about what worked well in the meeting and what didn't go as planned whilst it is still fresh, and to ensure that learnings from Effectiveness Reviews are embedded in practice and become habitual.

Good self-reflection practice includes: *What was required from the board and did it happen? What was missed? Were all agenda items captured?* and addresses not just *what* the board is doing, but *how* it is doing them.

Done well, reflection time allows the board to talk about whether they feel things are working and their contribution is valued, heading off frustrations before they become an issue.

This is even more important when things actually do go wrong.

*"Navel-gazing after things go wrong should be built into the agenda. There should be spot checks, rather than arse-covering. The trouble is that it is often not psychologically safe and gaslighting occurs after a crisis as people try to cover their tracks, glossing over something genuinely damaging: it wasn't **really** a crisis. Let's adopt the black box approach in aviation and focus on the problem, not the who"*

MANAGING BLACK SWANS AND GRAY RHINOS

Using the board's experience to think outside the box can be valuable. Some chairs think creatively to include areas that don't fall under conventional board scrutiny, whilst others work with the CEO to brainstorm relevant blue-sky discussion topics.

"Consider the 'Gray Rhino' - the big risk that is looming right in front of you, fuming, that hasn't done its damage yet but is an ever-present threat. It could be staff burnout, investment performance, commercial strategy"

Pre-mortem discussions can also be very powerful at averting potential disaster, by projecting failure and working backwards to imagine the causes and hence reduce the likelihood.

A Riot of Colours

5. BOARD COMPOSITION

5.1 SUMMARY

1. The chair sets the culture for the board and the company. A culture of trust and respect enables people to disagree and debate constructively, creating a safe space to admit, and hence address, knowledge gaps

2. Board chemistry is the magic 'je ne sais quoi' that makes a group of individuals greater than the sum of its parts. A board of highly talented individuals can perform less well than a board of less able individuals simply because they don't gel well

3. Chemistry can't be forced or predicted, but certain factors can help it to exist: respect; a balance of experience and freshness; the dynamic between the NEDs and the executive team; trust

4. Board dinners are a valuable way to help build chemistry and trust in a less formal setting, and to test the waters to help difficult boardroom conversations achieve constructive outcomes

5. There are no formal training or CPD requirements to be a NED, nor regular use of board coaches. These could be easy wins to increase board effectiveness

6. Hiring new NEDs is not as rigorous a process as hiring executives, with the focus often being on skills and experience, rather than strengths, fit and potential value-add

7. Extensive referencing can help to reduce the left tail risk of hiring someone who will be a bad fit. It is much harder to increase the right tail upside of hiring someone who will be a fabulous fit[5]

8. Getting diversity onto boards is a major focus. It is important to distinguish between cognitive diversity - so important for good decision making - and visible diversity - crucial for social signalling, inclusion and equality

9. Small boards are more effective, but the minimum size is determined by the complexity of the business and the need to staff committees. Not-for-profits and public companies tend to have larger boards

10. The optimal mix of NEDs to execs varies with the maturity of the business, more NEDs being needed as the business grows. There is a balance to be struck with having sufficient executive membership to have the expertise in the room, whilst ensuring NEDs can still challenge and provide oversight. On average, a ratio of 70:30 NEDs to execs is preferred

---

[5] Tail risk is the chance of a loss occurring due to a rare event, as predicted by a probability distribution

5.2 CULTURE

Organisational culture comes from the top. And that is no less true in the boardroom. The chair sets the tone for meetings, for the comport of the directors and their interactions with each other, the execs and for the business as a whole.

Great cultures prize honesty, integrity and respect, diversity and inclusivity. These aspects are particularly important in a boardroom: an open, inclusive, respectful debate where it is psychologically safe to be vulnerable allows people to operate confidently within their bounds of expertise.

Fig 5.1 - Bad Cultures
Copyright © 2020 Jenny Segal
Building Better Workplace Cultures 2020 Reference Group

A safe environment is particularly crucial given that board directors are hired for their skills and experience. They need to be able to admit to their limits, and where they require assistance. Whilst everyone is, and should be, encouraged to express their view, not all views should be weighted equally when knowledge is lacking, particularly when the matter under discussion is technical.

> *"The boardroom is like the family. You can speak your mind and everyone knows your heart is in the right place. The chair and the chief exec need to create this culture"*

So the culture needs to encourage robust, respectful debate in a safe environment. Setting the standard for boardroom conduct ensures a high bar for the quality and timeliness of papers, the professionalism of the directors' preparation, the richness of the debate, the post-meeting follow-up and intra-board interactions.

5.3 CHEMISTRY

> *"There are lots of wonderful people who just shouldn't be on the same board as each other. You can usually - with care - avoid appointing people who won't interact correctly. But chemistry is intangible. You can get rid of the left tail, but you can't engineer the right[6]"*

> *"It's the alchemy. The people, the context, the environment. It can be in the coming together to face a threat: the Financial Crisis. COVID"*

A board is not simply a collection of quality individuals with relevant experience, skills and strengths. A board is a team. The interactions between its members should create something powerful, something greater than the sum of its parts. That is where chemistry comes in. Good chemistry results in total cohesion: no point scoring, having your colleagues' back and wanting each other to succeed.

---

[6] Left tail is underperformance, whilst right tail is performance above expectations

> *"If someone doesn't quite fit, say they are significantly more argumentative, people can work around it. But it is a workaround. They can be coached, but not everyone is coachable"*

How the team gels is a very fine balance. On the one hand, there is no time to waste to get round personality clashes, so making sure people get on is really important. But if it gels too well, everyone can start to agree with each other, allowing complacency and groupthink to creep in.

Case Study: Too Cosy

One board I sat on recognised that they had grown too comfortable in each other's company and that they had developed a problem with groupthink. They discussed it transparently and decided to change the board's composition, identifying where there were skills overlaps to inform the succession planning.

At the other end of the spectrum, if a board doesn't gel at all, dysfunctional factions develop and conflict can derail decisions and prevent progress.

Boards should welcome curiosity. People should not be criticised for speaking out. There needs to be enough glue, whilst allowing for different perspectives, creative tension and grit in the system, to push the boundaries and the art of the possible. Neither comfortable boards nor infighting boards perform.

> *"How a board gels becomes very important when you get into a fight, eg with the government or with another company. You need to build up trust in advance. It gets tested under fire. You need to feel solid"*

There is an alchemy and mystique to creating board chemistry. What are the contributing factors?

RESPECT

> *"Seldom do people's views change during the meeting, but they should come with an open mind"*

> *"Be a truth-seeker, challenge. But do it thoughtfully and respectfully"*

Sometimes people are hired because they are a great personality fit, but they turn out to be useless. You don't need to all love each other. What you do need is mutual respect.

> *"Chemistry is more about how you push your opinions, about not dismissing people you believe to be misguided. It becomes a problem when people feel cowed so that they don't speak up or are too meek; irritability is a sign of stress and doesn't have a place in the boardroom."*

Disrespectful behaviour should be called out and handled sensitively by the chair.

> *"Simply saying 'I don't agree that...' is a point of conflict. If you are sitting on a nice, convivial board, you start to worry whether they will fire you. It doesn't feel good to challenge"*

> *"One negative individual causes controversy in the way they make points, although their points are good. The chair has marked that individual's card"*

Modesty, generosity and praise go a long way to demonstrate respect.

> *"It's about achieving good outcomes for stakeholders, not proving you are the smartest person in the room"*

> *"Give people credit: 'X said this a year ago', 'Y's idea..', shows that you value other peoples' perspectives"*

And sometimes the most awkward colleagues can surprise on the upside:

> *"The people who have been the most difficult to date have proved to be more adaptable than their more collegial colleagues"*

NEW BLOOD

It's important to get the balance right between new and old blood, so on balance the board is neither stale nor too experienced. Ideally, you don't want to have too many new people joining at the same time, so it is helpful to plan when directors roll on and off.

> *"The old-style, hands-off NED is on the wane. The new-style is more engaged"*

NED V EXEC

The chemistry between the board and the executives is critical. On the best boards, NEDs can communicate with the whole exec, not just the CEO; this requires a bond of trust so that the CEO is not threatened when directors access the wider team. A healthy chair/ CEO relationship enables the exec to be critiqued constructively; it goes horribly wrong if things get personal.

> *"The Regulator consistently asks for NEDs' challenges to be minuted. But this feels adversarial and that's not how it should be. Questioning, yes. But it skews NEDs towards being a bit spikey"*

People have got to get on, but the NEDs must not be in the exec's pockets. One of the biggest risks is NEDs being around for too long and going native so that they lose their independence and can no longer challenge.

TRUST

> *"When a board knows itself well and has established trust, it is parallel to a marriage. You can get a lot done when protocols are sorted"*

Building trust is a process and it starts with building rapport and establishing a personal bond. This is tricky if you only meet four times a year in a formal, board setting. Going through adversity together is a challenging but sure-fire way to shortcut the process.

> *"When you go through difficult times together - COVID, the portfolio value dropping - you really find out what your colleagues are like"*

A far more enjoyable way is via informal social gatherings.

> *"Trust is a big, hairy word. If you are challenging people, yours must be perceived as a valid viewpoint and not a personal threat. You first need to build a pool of social capital that most people call trust. This is best developed in person, without agenda, in an informal setting. Board dinners do this. They are not the only way, but they make sense in a time-challenged world"*

5.4 BOARD DINNERS ET AL

Boards exist to create challenge for the exec and to benefit stakeholders. For challenge to be constructive and productive, there needs to be an accumulated body of trust between the different parties. That is best fostered in an informal setting where colleagues can get to know each other.

BOARD DINNERS

"When you break bread with someone, you get to know them in a different way"

Board dinners are traditionally held the night before the quarterly board meeting, capitalising on board members being together and affording an opportunity to meet informally with or without the executive present, to reconnect, to discuss topics without them being minuted, to take the temperature for difficult conversations.

Are they old-fashioned or do they still have a place? I asked my reference group and they were overwhelmingly positive.

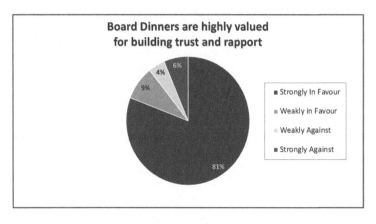

Figure 5.2 - Board Dinners Are Highly Valued

The general consensus is that the conviviality of board dinners makes a huge difference, and is possibly even vital, to building the quality of trust that makes disagreements easier and nurtures true team spirit. Their flavour varies from board to board, some holding dinners religiously every quarter and others less frequently. Some invite the whole executive team, whilst others keep it pure and restrict it to just the non-execs. Whatever their format and rhythm, a regular opportunity to get to know colleagues in a less formal setting was almost universally welcomed.

Case Study: The Warm-Up

The board dinner ensures you are all on the same page. It's about the politics you won't raise at the meeting.

It's the warm-up, the rehearsal, when you say the things you don't want minuted. It's perfect for airing those items that are much better said with alcohol.

This warm-up is really important, particularly if you haven't seen each other for a while. It gives you the opportunity to remember everyone: the characters, who knows what, who likes to speak first, how you gel as a team. You meet so infrequently, that it's crucial for the healthy dynamics of an effective board.

I underestimated it before COVID, but I really value it now.

There was a wider range of opinions around frequency and agenda. Some advocated fewer to avoid cluttering diaries and dinners becoming a mundane and monotonous chore.

Others preferred a specific purpose, such as a guest speaker or a discussion topic. And some preferred to hold them the night before, and others the night after, the meeting. Or in some cases, both:

> "Board dinners are super-valuable. On some of my boards, we hold them before and after the meeting. Before is good for clearing misconceptions and conflicts; it makes the meeting more effective. And it allows the introverts to express their opinions more easily. After ensures we are all on the same page for decisions made on the day. You can build the culture, trust and understanding, knowing that the work is done. And you can invite the exec and ask them additional questions"

Canny chairs make full use of the opportunity to tease out views and test the water on sensitive topics, particularly valuable if the dinner is the evening before the meeting. Their informal, cosy setting can create an openness and candour to tease out what people actually think. To say the unsayable.

> "It's important to have formal social events. If they are not organised formally, they will happen spontaneously; some people will get excluded and a sub-dynamic develops"

A few of my reference group were less positive about board dinners:

> "I hate the dinners that feel performative.
> I'm a mother. I book my car for 8:45pm and then leave"

> "Board dinners are old school. They're really not great if you don't drink wine, or if you have a young family. There is not the same level of creativity applied to organising workplace events"

> "I'm not a big fan of board dinners. Everyone is tired. You start making decisions before the board and there is a reason for board formality. But some non-board time is good. It could be unminuted conversations with no wine, no distractions, where you're allowed latitude in some of the statements you make"

but they all recognised the importance of spending time with each other informally outside of the boardroom setting. Perhaps having breakfast laid out in the room half an hour before the meeting starts to facilitate a friendly chat. Or scheduling adequate time for lunch and coffee breaks to allow people to socialise, as well as to eat and stretch their legs.

> *"Spending time together is invaluable and we utilise it well. It doesn't need to be a jolly"*

> *"Creating the space to build relationships is important. It eases the flow of conversation, picks up tricky personal issues, increases the ability to take risks in a conversation"*

I asked my participants what other formats their boards employ to get the team together informally. These tend to involve some aspect of strategy development and/or training, with board dinners as the sole purely-social setting.

FIELD TRIPS

Travelling together really helps to facilitate team bonding and the external stimulus can prompt innovative, blue-sky thinking. Field trips might extend to R&D, visiting customers, competitors and other countries, or time with the regulator. They might address something that is relevant now or they may be sowing the seeds for the future. It circumvents complacency, thinking what would and could be valuable for the board as a collective and as individuals.

> *"We would hold walking board meetings. All seven of us would meet up and go for a two to three hour hike. When you're walking next to someone, you have better conversations"*

STRATEGY DAYS

Many boards hold strategy days and my reference group found them helpful for standing back, pausing and seeing the bigger picture. Some include presentations from less well-known parts of the business and afford an opportunity to get exposure to the next levels of seniority down. Some invite suppliers or customers along. Others use them for facilitated team-building exercises, or for personality profiling.

WORKSHOPS

Some boards arrange workshops in which external speakers who have experienced a relevant challenge share their learnings. They can also be used for training on specialist niche topics, such as mental health and AI, or to run crisis management exercises.

> *"We do a lot of training together, typically four days a year. We get external providers in and we have covered a range of topics including legal, AI, cybersecurity and consumer duty"*

5.5 TRAINING

There are no formal training requirements to be a NED. Should there be?

> *"No-one trains you on how to be on a board. There is no competence threshold, no exams, no minimum standards. This is at odds with how important the role is for stakeholders, plus the fact that you are taking on personal liability. I did the FT NED diploma and found it really useful. I'm surprised more people don't do it and that is not looked for as part of the recruitment process"*

> *"It is very difficult for NEDs to be open about their training needs. It can happen when the chemistry is good and the environment feels safe, but you need to be very confident to make personal disclosures of your 'weaknesses': NEDs are dining out on their experience, not their vulnerabilities"*

INDUCTION

> *"Good boards will have an induction programme to get new NEDs up to speed, incorporating formal check-ins with the chair to course-correct and to help them spot things in the culture and make sure they're not missing things. It's especially valuable for first time NEDs"*

Several of my reference group spoke of their difficulties stepping into a new NED role, wanting to be additive from the start and not being a drag on the group. It takes about a year for new directors to feel comfortable; one-on-one calls or coffees with other board members and friendly guidance can speed up the process. It is important that they are cut some slack by their colleagues - and by themselves.

> *"Your personal effectiveness as a NED increases with the length of time you've served on the board"*

> *"When you go in, don't try to be a know-all on day one. Do the prep and don't be shy about asking questions and following up"*

CPD

Most professions have a requirement for ongoing development and learning, via formal and informal CPD[7]; this is not the case for NEDs. Perhaps there is a case for its introduction, with support provided by the organisation on whose board the NED serves. It could be adopted relatively quickly if it was screened-for in the recruitment process and reviewed as a periodic agenda item.

BOARD COACHES

Few boards make regular use of coaches, although some use them sporadically at strategy days. A permanent board coach could facilitate reflection on decision-making, culture and effectiveness in a more focused, professional way.

5.6 HIRING

"Start with skills, and hope for chemistry"

"Getting the chair right is key. You really don't want to get that wrong. It's very difficult to get rid of them"

Case Study: Scandinavian Boards

In Scandinavia, the board's chair is also the chair of the Nominations Committee. But the rest of the Nominations Committee is comprised of representatives from the largest shareholders, not the board directors. So the owners hold sway in appointing directors.

---

[7] Continuing Professional Development

Businesses spend a great deal of time recruiting their senior executives, a process often taking many months and involving multiple rounds of interviews. By comparison, hiring NEDs can feel quite light touch, particularly given they are typically in post for three consecutive three-year terms.

Getting recruitment right is tough. It is very hard to know what people are going to be like in a boardroom setting based on one or two short interviews. Ideally, the board will interview a lot of candidates, but this takes time. Head-hunters can streamline the process, possibly applying similar psychometrics to those used in executive search to get beyond the basic: *Can they read complicated financial papers?* to the more subjective: *Can they listen? Can they ask questions in an assertive, non-aggressive way?*

> *"Would-be NEDs should be honest about what they do and don't know and like. That way, the chair can work out if they are a good match"*

> *"Weak boards are often inflexible. Being flexible is important. I'm always nervous of people who display too much certainty"*

Case Study: Hiring New Board Members 1

It's really important for our whole board to buy into a new NED. Once we are down to the final two candidates, a small group of us takes each of them out for dinner. Three-on-one feels like outnumbering; two-on-one is ideal, with the same two meeting both candidates. We then socialise the favourite candidate to the full board. Here we are looking for the negatives, the reasons not to hire rather than the reasons to hire. If there are any negatives, we go back to the drawing board.

THE MAKINGS OF A GREAT NED

"You don't need to be weapons-grade at everything. Laymen are useful. They can help avoid defaulting to conventional wisdom"

"I am technocratic about the board. I want the chair of remuneration to know about remuneration. So I look for technocratic skills, business insights, curiosity and a willingness to help. And self-discipline - you need people who know how to contribute sensibly"

"You want objectivity and big picture, but it's really unfair to be on a board where you don't understand the subject matter and the business"

Whilst some expressed a preference for hiring NEDs with strong technical skills, others favoured good generalists who can provide a broader lens. Technical expertise is crucial for populating certain committees (risk, audit), but can result in a proliferation of certain personality types.

A well-networked NED can be of great benefit to the board. If they have three or four other appointments, they can share the best knowledge and practices from their other boards, along with their market insights.

REFERENCES

Given the importance of building a good part-time team, spending time taking multiple soft, informal references can help weed out those candidates who really won't fit.

> **Case Study: The Importance of Referencing**
>
> I'm a massive fan of referencing extensively. People often overlook this; they only want good references for reinforcement bias. Once we were interviewing three people for two positions, all women. There was something not quite right about the one with the strongest CV, something odd about her body language and the way she was dressed. So we got informal references. They described her as a sociopath.

> *"For one role I applied for, the first referee black balled me. Fortunately for me, the chair took up fourteen references and the other thirteen were glowing"*

> *"I look for people who are cooperative and happily helpful, who will muck in when needed. But you only really find out what people are like when you work with them. These are long term appointments, typically seven to nine years, so personal recommendations become even more important. You all go down together. According to the law, the chair of the board is not my boss"*

SKILLS

Boards should have a clear picture of their collective skills and experience, an understanding of who brings what to the table. Identifying skills gaps, coupled with emerging needs resulting from the strategic direction of the business, highlights where the skills hiring focus should be when there is turnover on the board.

Not every skills gap needs to be plugged with permanent board expertise though, and many boards bring in expert advisers to discuss particular technical issues. And this helps to manage the risk that when there is an 'expert' on the board, everyone relies on them and doesn't question their view.

> *"Some NEDs are super-smart. They may not say much, but it really counts; they ask the deep questions. If that person is leaving, look to replace someone with a similar style of intervention. Really smart chairs notice that"*

5.7 SKILLS V STRENGTHS

Chairs of well-run boards think very carefully about the **skills** they are losing when a director departs. The commonly-adopted 'skills matrix' systematically identifies the skills needed across the board and which are present in the existing directors, a gap analysis revealing those that would ideally be plugged via a cunning appointment. Often the scoring system is skewed towards the more quantitative *'Years of Experience'*, rather than the more subjective (but appropriate) *'Likes it and is good at it'*. But nonetheless this is a very sensible, and very actionable, approach.

> *"I've never really seen skills maps work effectively. Should we be hiring someone as the prima donna on a topic - for example, AI, the new buzz thing - or would it be better just to hire a consultant and raise everyone's knowledge? If I were writing a thesis on board composition, I would definitely include a skills map in my answer because the professors marking the paper would expect it, but then they've probably never sat on a board"*

BOARD SKILLS MATRIX			
	Director 1	Director 2	Average
Business Business Management Client Service Distribution Financial HR Investor Relations IT M&A Marketing Remuneration Risk Management Strategic Leadership Suppliers			
TOTAL:			
Investment Management Assets - Bonds Assets - Equities Assets - Liquid Alternatives Assets - Private Equity Assets - Property Compliance ESG Operations Portfolio Construction Risk Management			
TOTAL:			
Governance DE&I Corporate Governance Ethics Legal			
TOTAL:			
International UK Asia Pac Europe US			
TOTAL:			
GRAND TOTAL:			

Figure 5.3 - Typical Board Skills Matrix

Hiring for skills is particularly important for a younger business, where a nascent executive team lacks experience and looks to their NEDs for input and guidance. For a more seasoned company, the requisite skillset is often present in the business, so recent hands-on experience is less important for NEDs, who are there more for their oversight, guidance and wisdom.

But skills are only one part of the equation. NEDs also bring qualitative strengths to the table. Some might be great on strategy and others the finer detail, some might be extraordinary networkers, or very creative, or exhibit high levels of empathy. It is arguably just as important to have a balanced mix of these. How much thought are boards giving to hiring for strengths?

Very little, it transpires. Although one NED in the reference group spoke compellingly of how their board prioritises strengths in their hiring process:

Case Study: Strengths Analysis

We use a 'Strengths Finder' analysis as part of our recruitment process. Once we have got down to the final candidates, they complete a 45-minute online questionnaire to determine their strengths. All of our board members have been through this process and so we are conscious of each other's strengths. We found our board was heavy on 'Ideas' and 'Strategy', we had some 'Connectedness' but we were short of 'Implementation' strengths. We have found this a very useful approach.

It is really hard to identify strengths and there is heavy reliance on the recruitment process, head-hunters and references. But inevitably you only see part of the person. Fireside chats with each board member can help to piece together a broader picture, as can reading through their social media postings. A useful touchpoint is looking back at a candidate's executive career; if they rose to a senior position in a business whose culture you know, you may well have a view of what they needed to do to succeed in that environment.

A complementary way to seek a balance of strengths is through diversity.

5.8 DIVERSITY

> *"Diversity should be an asset, not a problem. Not just there because someone's told you you need it on a board"*

> *"The world is made up of a plethora of individuals and the Board should reflect that. We will see the benefit in the next five to ten years as women and ethnic minorities come into their own"*

A thorny question faces those holidaying in the West Country that threatens the tranquility of a summer's afternoon:

*jam before cream,
or cream before jam?*

Cornish folk favour the former, whilst denizens of Devon know that cream is like butter so it goes on first.

Jam Before Cream or Cream Before Jam?

Navigating entrenched views such as these is an art and a science. Involving a good mix of people is widely acknowledged to lead to better decisions and helps avoid the demon groupthink: diversity can help to synthesise new thinking, allowing us to circumvent enduring disagreement or ghastly compromise.

However, introducing diversity will alter the board dynamics. The benefits are clear in terms of being socially equitable and avoiding groupthink, but there may well be a trade-off between ease-of-proceedings and the heterogeneity we seek through ED&I[8].

> *"I can really see why the Old Boys' Network worked. You know what you're getting, and that's really valuable. But how do we bring in wonderful, rich diversity?"*

And what do we actually mean by diversity? **Visible diversity** has an important role to play, but it extends beyond the physicality of how people present to the outside world to capturing different ways of thinking: true **cognitive diversity**. Nuclear physicists and theologians will approach a problem very differently.

How should we ensure we appropriately represent, and benefit from, diversity in a boardroom context? And with some boards still hiring in the image of the chair, what progress is being made towards achieving diversity?

> *"I brought in the former CEO of The Wine Society. He had a great interest in English language and wanted the communications to be clearer"*

---

[8] Equality, Diversity and Inclusion

> **Case Study: The Congenial Boys' Club**
>
> I sat on a board where pretty much everyone had the same mindset. It was like a congenial boys' club and I was the only woman. It was pretty lonely and it made it very difficult to raise an alternative point of view: the hurdle to challenge was much higher and the quality of discussion not so rich. It resulted in a lot of groupthink and a blurring of purpose.

VISIBLE DIVERSITY

> *"Main committees are still largely chaired by white blokes"*

Whilst quotas and ratios can be an irritating overlay when you are trying to find the best skills for the job, they serve an important purpose in social signalling, showing that it is possible for people from various background and ethnicities to succeed. Some in my reference group felt that quotas relating to ethnicity are unrealistically high and should instead reflect the proportions present in key stakeholder populations.

> *"It shouldn't be about a quota; it should be about who is the best for the job. Ask how many people from these backgrounds have the requisite skills"*

However, quotas do get results. A lot of boards have now achieved a 50:50 male/female split, although most struggle to achieve ethnic minority representation.

But they have their drawbacks.

It can be harder to get a range of high-quality candidates when there is a diversity hurdle to meet. The counter view is that you just need to cast the net wide enough. Plus there is often intersectionality between minority groups, such as social mobility and race, allowing a board to benefit from several dimensions of diversity with just one hire. Sometimes compromise might be required, for example relaxing a requirement to hire a former CFO, but with a little creativity it should not be a problem.

> *"I believe in an abundance mentality - that people from diverse backgrounds with the right skills do exist. They are not mutually exclusive. It's just harder to find them"*

Quotas can also lead to imposter syndrome, with the appointee worrying they have received a leg-up and were not necessarily the best candidate for the job, whilst other board members assume they were only appointed to tick a box.

COGNITIVE DIVERSITY

> *"Diversity of thought is very important and is every bit as important as visible diversity. One board is full of 60-year-old bald guys, but they all have different career backgrounds. The IT guy has secret contracts with MI6"*

Studies[9] on cognitive diversity demonstrate that if you have a group of subject matter experts and a group of cognitively diverse individuals, the latter wins in decision-making quality. But the trouble is, it is much, much harder to identify cognitive diversity.

---

[9]   McKinsey & Co: 'Why Diversity Matters' (2015), 'Diversity Wins' (2020)

In the executive world, we map people into buckets - empathic, connective, logical, detailed, directive - and think about how they comport themselves and problem-solve. We have yet to see this take hold in the board world.

And cognitive diversity on its own is not sufficient. We need personalities that not only have different views but are contrarian enough to express them. Most people are not very brave and it is human nature not to feel comfortable in a minority.

INTERNATIONAL DIVERSITY

Simply introducing people of different nationalities can stimulate valuable debate and diverse views.

> *"The UK has a fantastic Stewardship Code. Yet there is no correlation between the Code and good corporate performance - quite the reverse. This makes international boards difficult and can create UK/US tensions and around issues like the US having a combined chair/CEO"*

> *"A bad board is where everyone agrees with each other. But the Brits hate disagreement! International boards are much more comfortable with debate. American, Dutch, Australian - cultural diversification leads to better debate. Boards **should** be uncomfortable, but respectful"*

> *"I've built Asian businesses for many years and I encountered very different ideas about the right way to contribute and to find ways to have effective outcomes. It was a lot of fun"*

NEURODIVERSITY

In her powerful **Chess Club - Drama Club** analogy, Sally Bridgeland has captured a simple way of expressing neurodiversity and the benefits these can confer in the boardroom.

Chess Club - Drama Club

Copyright © 2023 Jenny Segal

"As an introvert, I liked virtual meetings. I could put up my hand and be heard. Or I could put my comments in the chat. I'm braver now. But how do you get the best out of introvert chess club? When you're in the room, you need to be drama club"

Boardrooms are not a very neurodiverse or neurodiverse-friendly setting. Having dyslexia, for example, could effectively exclude you from being a NED because of difficulties in reading voluminous board papers. And this is a great loss because neurodiversity can lead to a much more interesting, effective discussion.

> "To truly capture cognitive diversity, we should be including neurodiverse candidates in the mix. One way to achieve this is to look for different routes of advancement and education. Creatives think differently. When we look at candidates' career profiles, there is a lot of homogeneity. Open this up and we will see more cognitive diversity coming through."

> "As an introvert, I'm less comfortable in smaller groups. I struggle to pick up non-verbal cues."

AGE

There are some interesting generational and demographic shifts developing in the boardroom. There is a welcome trend to hire younger people, but it is still important that they have relevant executive experience to ensure they are adding maximum value.

> "Many board members are older and will be timing out after nine years on a board. With the growing importance of AI, cyber and digital, it is likely that, net-net, younger people will be coming into the boardroom. This is bound to lead to a change in the way boards operate, away from the current set-up of formality, typically with a 70-year-old, white male chair. How will those two worlds collide? What happens when the chair is 20 years younger than the NEDs, à la Mark Zuckerberg?"

POLITICAL CORRECTNESS

We talk a lot about bringing our authentic selves to work. But in a world of increasing political correctness, it can be hard to strike the right balance. And this can affect the quality of debate possible in the boardroom.

> *"We need to be tolerant of different points of view. There is a real danger that PC-ness leads to groupthink. University debating societies can no longer tolerate different points of view. If we project forward a few years, there will be people who are unable to engage in constructive debate, where debate is absent. These people will be future board members. We need to combat this. People are disinvited, cancelled. It is creeping into the boardroom"*

> *"We now have a defined vocabulary which we are required to use for DE&I. Yet there are some things you have to be able to talk about when you are trying to protect your business' reputation. And you don't want it minuted, but you do want to be able to air the thought to aid people's understanding. Yet you can't. It's like operating under a medieval blasphemy law"*

> *"We talk about bringing our true selves to work, but what is the world ready to accept? How would my boardroom colleagues react if I turned up wearing traditional dress?"*

5.9 SMALL IS BEAUTIFUL

Boards have got big. There are so many boxes to be ticked to meet regulatory requirements and to man the necessary committees, and some boards have expanded further to include the requisite mix of gender and ethnic diversity. Yet most people in my reference group expressed a strong preference for small boards.

> *"Boards should be as small as possible and as large as necessary to cover the bases"*

> "With larger boards, there's a free-rider problem. If you're one of 15, your individual contribution is so small, you can switch off and it won't be noticed. Smaller boards force you to make the effort and take responsibility"

HOW TO KNOW IF THERE ARE TOO MANY PEOPLE IN YOUR MEETING

It may be easy to default to inviting a crowd of people to a meeting — that way, you don't really have to identify the most critical participants, you'll avoid any ruffled feathers, you'll have everyone involved on hand for a decision, and you won't have to repeat your communications separately afterwards. Or maybe your tendency is to want to keep things small: you may be tempted to invite just a small group of people whose opinions you most value.

But for a meeting to be useful, you have to have the right people — and only the right people — in the room. With too many attendees, you may have trouble focusing everyone's time and attention and accomplishing anything; with too few, you might not have the right decision makers or information providers in the room.

– from 'Running Meetings', Harvard Business Review (2014)

Harvard Business Review's research suggests:

- **for problem-solving or decision-making, invite no more than eight people. With more, there is too much conflicting input;**

- **for brainstorming, up to around 18 is effective;**

- **for an update meeting, there is no upper limit unless everyone is providing an update, in which case limit it to 18; and**

- **for rallying the troops, the sky is the limit.**

In other words, communication degrades once a group numbers more than eight, and it stops being a conversation at all once it grows to 18. At that point, the chair needs to be more directive: "Here are 17 views and this is the answer we're going with".

> *"It becomes counterproductive to have too many people; more than 10, and the permutation of interactions is too complicated and the level of ownership decreases dramatically"*

> *"The size of board is only one side of the story. How many other people are in the room? I sit on a board of 12 that has 10 more attending"*

So how should we think about optimal board size?

OPTIMAL SIZE

The "right" size is a function of various factors.

Complexity. Simple businesses need fewer board members. Investment trusts, for example, often have as few as four. The optimal size grows with the complexity of the business, the breadth of specialist knowledge required, the number of sub-committees, the purpose of the board and the number of stakeholders.

> *"Investment Trust boards are small. One I sat on had four; that was too small. If two are friends and appoint a third that is also their friend, challenge is impossible"*

> *"The minimum size is often driven by the need to staff committees. You need a minimum of five: the four chairs (Main, Audit, Risk, Remuneration & Nominations) plus a spare. The spare is the only way you'll get diversity as you have to mirror the exec team you're facing off against: you need an ex-CEO as a chair, an accountant to chair Audit, a former Chief Risk Officer to chair Risk and an HR person as the Rem & Nom chair"*

Size. Start-ups typically have fewer directors, growing their board as the business scales. For small and medium-sized enterprises (SMEs), the ideal size is probably around three to five directors as committees are often unnecessary.

Not-for-profit boards are larger, as they represent every stakeholder. This can result in more disengagement and less focus.

> *"On charity boards, meetings often won't be at their full complement. There is just not the same level of commitment: holidays take precedence. In the quoted world, board meeting attendance is a priority because of the associated disclosures"*

Public companies tend to have larger boards than private companies, often reflecting greater regulation and more stakeholders.

> *"There is a huge difference between private and public boards. The incentives are different on public boards - there are different drivers and more random individuals. Some can be very good, some can be an enormous distraction. You get special interest groups. And it is very difficult to remove people. On private boards, people tend to be very driven, often focused on floating the business in x years' time"*

5.10 IN THE MIX

What is the right balance between NEDs and executives? This varies with the longevity of the business with younger businesses requiring more executive input, their need for NEDs growing as they mature.

However, having just a few NEDs on a board makes it difficult for them to function effectively because it is harder to challenge the executive from a minority position.

> *"You need a minimum of three NEDs for them to be useful. One pair of external ears is good, but three encourages them to step up and you're not the only one who doesn't understand the business. The exec is in the know and can exclude a sole NED"*

Some advocate a 50:50 split to ensure there is enough domain knowledge in the room whilst still allowing the NEDs to feel empowered to challenge; others think this confuses and that a majority of NEDs is essential. But if the purpose of the board is oversight and holding the exec to account, this requires a majority of NEDs. Yet some CEOs like to invite their team onto the board to keep them happy and recognise their contribution. So how many executives should there be?

> *"All the C-suite should attend the board. I'm less bothered if, say, the head of distribution is actually on the board, but they do need to be there. It helps to see the quality of the team, for succession planning and to get a sense of the balance between the CEO and the rest of the team. It's dangerous if everything is filtered through the CEO and the CFO"*

> *"There is a risk you get a load of NEDs with axes to grind and little knowledge of business who don't get the pressures the exec team is under"*

> "There can be little doubt that the current system has directly led to the failure or chronic underperformance of many businesses, including banks, supermarkets and pubs.
>
> I believe by vesting so much power in non-executive directors, the system is also disenfranchising executives and the workforce – the people who have real expertise and are the cornerstone of business success"
>
> **– Tim Martin, Founder and Chair of Wetherspoons**
> *from Wetherspoons' trading update, 13th November 2019*

There is a common view that there should be more than one executive on the board so they can back each other up, with the CEO and CFO as a minimum. But the jury is out on whether this is sufficient or whether there should be broader executive membership.

Arguments in favour include the board having access to the people who know where the big risks are and the bodies are buried, and bringing the exec into the circle of accountability. Cynics suggest it is a handy ploy to improve the gender diversity statistics.

Those arguing against are keen to avoid blurring the distinction of the role of the board and the exec function.

> *"You almost need man-to-man marking, one NED for each executive function. Although this is expensive and duplicative"*

> *"The higher the board is in the governance structure - when it is dealing with strategy and executive evaluation - the more NEDs are needed, typically around two-thirds. Closer to the battlefield, it's more tactical, so you need more executives"*

Case Study: Subsidiary Boards

There can be tremendous pressure from head office when you serve on a subsidiary board. For UK subsidiaries, the UK board runs the operation and is governed by UK regulatory regime, not that of the home country of head office. Maintaining that understanding can be politically difficult, particularly if the UK CEO has been parachuted in on a secondment from head office.

The board size is typically six, made up of two execs from head office, two local execs and two NEDs. The execs from head office can make it very difficult, so you really need more NEDs to function effectively.

The views of those in my reference group who would be drawn on the optimal numbers are shown below:

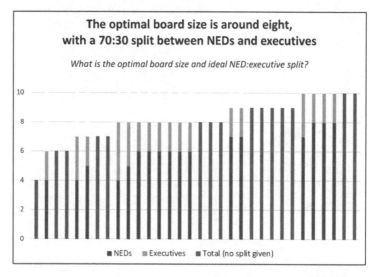

Figure 5.4 - Optimal Board Size

The Beverage You Are About To Enjoy Is Extremely Hot

Copyright © 2023 Jenny Sega

6. BOARD PAPERS

6.1 SUMMARY

1.   Widely used and great for sharing information, board portals are an easy and confidential way to distribute board packs. However, they can lead to a lack of discipline around the length of the pack and the timeliness of its delivery, there are still plenty of directors who prefer to read a hard copy and it is too easy to scroll through virtual papers without properly absorbing them

2.   Board packs are far too long. There are many reasons for this: a desire for transparency, poor understanding of how to structure a board paper, lack of clarity of purpose, execs trying to demonstrate their knowledge levels, execs not wanting/being able to dedicate resource to produce fit-for-purpose documents or a deliberate ploy to bury detail

3.   Long papers are unhelpful. Not only is it difficult to see what's important, but the regulator will assume that all parts of the board pack have been read and factored into decision-making

4. The perfect paper has a cover sheet including a title, a headline, an executive summary and a call to action for the board. The main body of the paper is clear and concise. All the detailed workings are in the appendix and it should be assumed that this will be unread unless a director has a particularly deep interest

5. Sending out papers too late for them to be read properly is a common mistake. Using a company secretariat function to streamline pack production, or looking to move the board meetings out by a few days to give more time after the quarterly reporting is available, can help to relieve the pressure

6.2 BOARD PORTALS

Board portals are commonplace now for the dissemination of board packs.

Whilst they come in several shapes and sizes, they all have similar functionality, allowing attendees to share annotations and comments, to post articles and to deal with items ahead of time that don't have to be dealt with synchronously and waste valuable board air space. They force consistency and create a single source of truth. And they do away with the need for printing out and binding reams and reams of paper, improving security and helping to save the planet in the process.

However, there are drawbacks:

> *"Older people prefer paper"*

a view expressed by a number of the younger members of my reference group too.

> *"It's much easier to correct minutes on paper. I used to be able to circle my comments and hand in the ripped-out page. It's much harder to give feedback on a virtual deck"*

> *"Some boards are resistant to printing out hard copies and I've struggled to get a set. But it's just too easy to scroll and not read the papers when they're on a screen."*

They also remove a certain element of discipline around board pack production. Because packs are no longer printed and bound, there is not the same barrier to adding in additional papers last minute, as it is all too easy just to drop them into the portal. But the receiving NEDs get their papers by drip feed, which is less than ideal - no-one wants an unpredictably endless stream of materials.

And they have also removed an upper limit for the length of board papers.

> *"When everything was typed, you didn't get 1,400 pages"*

From 'THE HITCH-HIKER'S GUIDE TO THE GALAXY'

"But the plans were on display…"

"On display? I eventually had to go down to the cellar to find them."

"That's the display department."

"With a flashlight."

"Ah, well, the lights had probably gone."

"So had the stairs."

"But look, you found the notice, didn't you?"

"Yes," said Arthur, "yes I did. It was on display in the bottom of a locked filing cabinet stuck in a disused lavatory with a sign on the door saying 'Beware of the Leopard'. Ever thought of going into advertising?"

– Douglas Adams

Board papers have got very long.

Packed with detail, spreadsheets, analysis, balance sheets, models, they can number 1,000 pages or more. The trouble is, with so much information it can be hard to see what is actually important. And, given board members often have a week at best to read the papers, it can seem an impossible task doomed to failure which encourages skim reading.

> *"It's too easy to drop documents into virtual board packs, so there isn't the same bar for inclusion as in the days when they were printed out. And you can never be expected to read a 1,000-page document, so it legitimises not reading them"*

> *"The real litmus test question is: 'If you could only submit 5 pages out of the 80, what would they say?'"*

For regulated businesses, there is the additional risk that if something is included in the board pack, the regulator will expect you to have read it and take it into account in your decision-making. They may even question you about it in years to come. Even if it was buried on page 984 in size 6 font.

> *"The Exec thinks that having everything in the board pack is helpful. It's not! It's not about the Exec showing off about how much they know or how much work they've done. If it's in the board paper, in 20 years' time a board member can be quizzed on why there was a number on p387 that they didn't challenge"*

> *"The FCA[10] can question you on the main papers, but it's harder to question you on papers in the appendices. For every two days of meetings, I spend three days preparing, yet I will tell FCA that I don't have time to read everything. I'm there to challenge, not to go through all the detail"*

The level of detail can be driven from a good place - a desire to be transparent and to share all the facts. It can also arise from a misplaced desire to demonstrate to the board how competent the author is:

---

[10] Financial Conduct Authority

> *"Boards are checking that you're the right person and you are doing your stuff. An overly-detailed paper is a red flag that the person doesn't know what is or isn't important"*

Sometimes it is a legacy from poor time-management in past meetings:

> *"Over time, board paper length adapts to how well-run the meeting is. If there is not enough time to discuss topics, execs will start to assume they will only get five minutes instead of their advertised 20. So they will write longer papers as they will assume they won't get the opportunity to make their points live"*

There can also be a lack of understanding from the executive about how a board paper should be set out; stylistically, it is very different from the structure necessary to inform executive decision-making. It could simply have been written for the wrong audience, showing the workings rather than simply summarising the issue and stating what is required of the board. And sometimes it is just easier to recycle executive-style papers, particularly if there isn't a company secretariat function to share the paper production workload.

Verbose papers can reflect a poor exec-NED dynamic, with the exec team hiding stuff in the detail to get it through without debate. Or if there is a perception that the board doesn't add value, the exec may be unwilling to go to all the extra effort.

Occasionally a paper is too short, with insufficient explanation to be able to get the context and narrative.

> *"There is a big difference between slides and PowerPoint - the latter is not a short-cut and summarises too much"*

As a rule, a lot of work goes into the production of board papers and it's important that the responsible executive gets recognised.

6.4 THE PERFECT PAPER

> *"Rarely is the important point in the detail. The risk is you miss something that's hiding in plain sight"*

> *"Write for a five-year-old Beano reader"*

> *"There is a chess club - drama club balance to be struck in the perfect board paper. You need enough detail to demonstrate the quality of the analytics, but you need the story to bring it alive: you're paying a lot of money for the people to be in the room so you don't want to waste their time"*

Peeling Back the Layers

Copyright © 2023 Jenny Segal

The best board papers are like an onion. You peel back the layers to get more and more detail and you can stop when you've seen enough.

HOW TO STRUCTURE A FANTASTIC BOARD PAPER

Too many board papers are overly long.
This paper proposes a format that solves the problem.

Executive Summary:

Papers should start with a clear summary sheet, comprising a title, a headline and then an executive summary. This should be followed with a "call to action" for the board: is the paper for noting, discussion and/or decision?

The main part of the paper should then follow, giving one or two layers of crisp, additional information supporting the exeuctive summary.

It should conclude with a clear list of recommendations, including the consequences of their adoption (and non-adoption).

Any workings, further detail and analytics: surverys of opinions, data etc supporting the main body of the paper, should be included in the appendix. Assume that no one reads the appendix, unless they have a deep interest in the topic.

Action Required:	Discuss the prinicples proposed Decide which ones to adopt
Main Content:	Use crisp, clear language, avoiding jargon. Give more explanation to support the recommendations, but don't go into too much detail! Keep it high level and don't show the workings or the supporting analytics - that should live in the appendix, not least because if it is in the main body the regulator will assume it was read and taken into account in the decision-making.
Recommendations:	Adopt this format! It will reduce the board pack to a maximum of 300 pages. If we continue with the status quo, the papers will continue to be too long and key points can get lost.
Appendices:	This is where to put the analytics, detailed workings, links to sources etc

Figure 6.1 - How To Structure A Fantastic Board Paper

There should be a cover page at the front, with a heading and a paragraph in bold setting out at the highest level what the issue is and what you need to do about it (noting / discussion / decision). The rest of the page is an executive summary, written by the responsible executive so you get a sense of their voice.

Then there are a couple more pages with further information and the detail is in the appendix with links you can click on if you have a deep interest. But you should be able to see from the front page what it's all about; the rest is for an interested reader.

> *"Summaries at the front are a blessing and a curse.*
> *They encourage skimming of the paper"*

Case Study: The External Opinion

We invite external experts in every three years to review the quality of our papers. They point out the obvious stuff: the paper's purpose should be clearly marked as: 'For Information' or 'For Decision', there should be a headline, an executive summary, and a note of how much time is needed to discuss them. And there should be an appendix for the detail.

And minutes weren't coming through quickly enough. We needed to take actions and decisions within 48 hours and to review the minutes within 10 working days, while the meeting was still relatively fresh.

PURPOSE

When the chair and the CEO are working together on the meeting agenda, they should strive for a clarity of purpose in the papers they commission from the executive team, being really clear about what they need and why.

> "When board members ask for more detail, they are worried about something. Often they don't actually want more detail, it is more a flag of concern"

> "Board papers are an art. When I was writing them as an exec, I always tried to see it from the NEDs' viewpoint. To give them enough information about what they are deciding. If a NED says, 'Do X, not Y', they don't know what the knock-on effect will be. They need to understand the implications of their decisions"

Strategic papers can and should be reasonably open-ended, citing strengths, weaknesses, challenges and a range of outcomes, whilst papers relating to more operational matters need to narrow down the options, make recommendations and drive decisions.

CLARITY

> "The papers are too jargony, especially the ones about Cyber and IT. Or they go to the other extreme and everything is expressed in analogies. Then the next lot give you different analogies. And you find yourself speaking back to them in analogies. Moats or Spears? No one is talking noughts and ones"

Using clear language is important.

"If I started to write elaborately...
I found that I could cut that scrollwork
or ornament out and throw it away..."

– Ernest Hemingway

Source: www.goodfreephotos.com

Obfuscation, jargon and waffle at best bury the points the paper is trying to bring out, and at worst sow insidious seeds that something material is being deliberately hidden, creating a lack of trust and damaging the NED-executive dynamic.

FORMAT

Board papers risk being Goldilocks-like: too much, too little, too dense, wrong font. Having some rules around their format can eliminate some of the frustrations systematically. And an easy and obvious win is to spell-check the papers: small errors cast doubt over the accuracy of the rest of the materials.

Some boards have adopted a standard font and layout so there is consistency across papers. A template that summarises the key issues - visual if possible - can help to emphasise the important points.

Others make good use of Red - Amber - Green dashboards incorporating the leading business and management risk indicators, helping to signal where the NEDs should focus attention.

Simple things, such as highlighting what has changed, where you can find something that has moved and following a consistent structure from pack to pack when presenting regular data items can all help reduce unhelpful dissonance.

6.5 DON'T BE LATE

Getting timeliness right is a big deal.

> *"The board pack always arrives too late, with the exec often working on papers until the eleventh hour. I build reading time into my week. If papers arrive late, or if there are late changes, I don't have time to read them. People don't have a whole day to prep and I can't read past 10pm at night"*

Simple but not easy, the papers need to be delivered sufficiently ahead of time for the board to have the opportunity to fully focus on them. Yet they also need to be sufficiently up-to-date to reflect the most recent developments in the business. It's a fine balance; perhaps shifting the board meeting dates out by a few days can achieve a workable compromise. And using a company secretariat function to produce papers can iron out some of the production wrinkles.

> *"The papers for my current board are awesome. But they used to be a shambles and we needed a dedicated resource to put them together"*

City Buzz

7. BOARD MEETINGS

7.1 SUMMARY

1. A mix of in-person and virtual meetings is ideal

2. In-person meetings are best for discussion that requires opinion, interaction and nuance, and for making difficult decisions

3. Virtual meetings are best for committee meetings, for task-based matters, for rapid decisions and for quick discussions, providing fantastic flexibility for last minute matters

4. People hate hybrid meetings. When joining remotely, you do not have equal footing in the meeting. If you have an important point to convey, you should attend in person

5. Keeping people's attention in virtual meetings can be tough. It can be aided by scheduling regular breaks and by adopting clear etiquette on how to behave in meetings

6. For virtual and hybrid meetings, the IT needs to work to avoid it becoming a major distraction and potentially derailing the meeting. Having IT support on hand, testing the kit beforehand and investing in the best kit can help to alleviate problems

7. Meetings can run better with an excellent company secretariat function, having a social chair, injecting a bit of levity and having a round boardroom table

8. Given the flexibility afforded by virtual meetings, it might be valuable to question the length and periodicity of board meetings to make them shorter and more frequent

7.2 TO ZOOM OR NOT TO ZOOM?

Prior to 2020, everybody was expected to attend every board and committee meeting in person. Exceptions were strictly by permission only. But the pandemic allowed us to develop a new way of working, introducing much more flexibility around how boards meet. I asked my reference group for their thoughts on the costs and benefits of this new-found flexibility.

> *"I recruited a whole board via Teams. The first year of meetings were all virtual. I thought it would be a shambles, totally ineffective. But it was fine"*

Having a range of ways to meet has brought many benefits. By intentionally matching purpose with format, meetings have become more focused and more effective.

There is still a strong desire to have regular meetings in person, so important for building trust, rapport and board cohesion, or when it is crucial to read body language. Virtual meetings are the perfect complement, ideal for discussing more technical matters, for committees and for quick meetings which need to be called at short order. And reducing in-person meetings rides the zeitgeist of the post-COVID appetite for travel, cost concerns and climate change. Plus, having the option to join remotely results in far fewer apologies.

It all sounds marvellous. So what's the catch?

People hate hybrid meetings.

> *"There is a tipping point. One person on the screen is fine, but once you get to, say, two or three on screen and six in the room, it becomes much harder. The people in the room have side chats and it gets worse as numbers grow"*

> *"It should be 100% zoom or 100% room"*

100% IN-PERSON

Face-to-face meetings are viewed as the most productive format for discussion that requires opinion, interaction and nuance. There needs to be tension and edginess for a board to work effectively, and in-person is a better environment for difficult conversations because you can read the body language, sense the leg-tapping under the table, and diffuse a situation over a coffee or a side-bar conversation.

> *"We need to practice conflict. Conflict is a muscle that we need to exercise in low stake environments. When the stakes are high, we become paralysed. People get offended and shut each other down. Everyone has a right to raise dissent - a good chair and a good board recognises the importance - and it's so much easier in an in-person setting"*

Engagement and concentration levels are higher when people meet in person:

> *"One board meeting lasts a day and a half! It is mind-numbing via zoom"*

> *"I've experienced one person not coming to anything in person because of personal circumstances. Their effectiveness has vastly diminished"*

and it is the most conducive for showing solidarity with a dissenting voice, for integrating new board members and for meeting the level down from the executive so as to aid succession planning.

100% VIRTUAL

However, virtual meetings are now viewed as essential. Not only do they provide flexibility, but they are much more efficient and effective for committee meetings, for task-based matters like approving the Report & Accounts, for rapid decisions during an M&A, for quick discussions or for pre-work so that when you get to the 'real life' meeting, a lot has been surfaced and the board can focus on the meat.

> *"I'm a big believer of using the screen share function so everyone can see the relevant pages of the topic being discussed"*

> *"Virtual is a blessing when sign-offs are required, or for last-minute meetings"*

> *"I really hate being asked to go somewhere for an hour"*

They do, however, require different chairing skills. It can be easier for people to be aggressive online and difficult to shut down the "chatty Cathys". The chair has to work harder to get input from everyone, to spot the signs that someone wants to speak and to tease out comments from the more reticent.

And it is very difficult to read the virtual room if the faces don't all fit on once screen. Because it is harder for everyone to pick up on non-verbal cues, it can also be harder for the chair to regain control over the agenda when people go off-piste.

Virtual meetings can be difficult if people have never met before in person. However, introverts often find them easier:

> *"Live, you're always waiting for a gap to make your point. There is less listening. The less-meek speak over the meek. The chair would often say I'd make a great point, but I made it too late, unravelling 10 minutes of debate. Online, everyone gets heard at the right time."*

> *"We got into the habit of putting up virtual hands when we want to speak. I found it helpful in getting heard over my more voluble colleagues"*

The trouble with hybrid meetings is that they are not a level playing field.

If a director chooses to join a hybrid meeting remotely, they know that they don't have the same place at the table. Protocols can help, but they are not fool-proof: if you really want to influence the discussion, you need to be physically present in the room.

> *"We were meeting in person to deal with a particularly sensitive matter. Then a train strike was announced and some people couldn't get there. So we decided to make the meeting 100% virtual as it was fairer'*

Hybrid meetings are universally regarded as the worst by a wide margin. Some boards dislike them so much that they make the people who are in the office sit in different rooms and dial in individually to make it a 100% remote meeting.

> *"Hybrid is completely ineffective. It is better not to join at all than to attend an in-person meeting remotely. Or, if you have to join to provide some crucial input, you do so for a very short period where you have the floor and then you dial out. Some circumstances - a crisis, or if international colleagues are joining - may demand a compromise. But it's not sustainable. It's unfair on everyone to attempt hybrid meetings"*

They are much, much harder for the chair, who must check in constantly to keep everyone involved or risk losing a range of opinions. The people in the room forget about the people on the screen and have side conversations. Unless the chair is brilliant, you end up having two meetings.

> *"I hate hybrid, particularly if I'm chairing"*

> *"Hybrid is convenient, but unsatisfactory. It is genuinely difficult to involve the subset on the screen - they can't hear, they typically can't see and they don't feel part of it. Is it better for them to join via zoom than miss the discussion? Maybe. But it causes disruption, particularly if they have dodgy Wi-Fi"*

However, plenty of global companies have been using hybrid meetings for years. And with discipline, etiquette protocols and mindful repositioning of the microphone, they can still be made to work.

> *"I am a Justice of the Peace and, in remote court hearings, it is very strict. People can't just stand up and walk away. They are not allowed to consume anything - just water - and they have to look at the camera when they are speaking. Businesses could learn a lot from this, as our discipline around remote meetings is lacking. It's a bit like when we first started to use emails: initially it was like sending a text, but now they've become quite formal"*

Some have co-opted the company secretary into a social chairing role to monitor the rooms - real and virtual - to make sure everyone is involved.

And hybrid meetings have opened the door to diversity, making it much easier for people with disabilities, or those who have mobility issues or who are geographically distant, to join boards.

7.3 TECHSTRACTION

There are some practical issues with joining a meeting virtually.

People get distracted by what's going on in their direct environment. Even with the best will in the world and when you think you've turned off all your notifications, your watch buzzes to let you know a message has arrived, or the cat comes in, or the doorbell rings.

And whilst businesses are very aware of how to mitigate the mental stresses and physical strains arising from being in the office, less thought is given to the frequency of breaks for those joining meetings virtually. Zoom fatigue is becoming increasingly recognised, and part of this is to do with eye strain and sitting in one place for several hours.

Then there is the question about attention span and whether those online remain engaged.

> *"We were quite imaginative at first about building in breaks when we were all virtual. It's harder to do when it's hybrid"*

> *"Men's average attention span is 11 minutes, women's is 16. Checking emails in meetings is ok. It's certainly better than making a disruptive comment"*

People have become addicted to their phones. And phone-checking habits have filtered through into in-person meetings in a way that would have been considered unacceptably rude pre-pandemic.

ETIQUETTE

One way to mitigate some of these issues is to be clear about what is expected, by defining and adhering to behaviour protocols. Etiquette is foundational and is evolving rapidly.

Setting expectations about the use of cameras is important. The protocol might require all attendees to keep theirs on at all times. Or it might require those attending as observers to have theirs switched off unless they are speaking, to help the chair manage the faces on screen.

Being clear about how to make a point is helpful - must it be via first raising a virtual hand, or are interruptions acceptable? Someone (the company secretary?) could be tasked with keeping an eye out for people coming off mute to anticipate when someone wants to contribute.

And then there is the age-old problem around how to handle tech malfunctions.

> *"I've always struggled with hybrid: the mics don't work properly, people online can't hear, one person's set-up causes an echo, people continuously muting and unmuting, poor internet connections. It's massively distracting. You wouldn't allow it in real life. The internet is just not reliable enough yet"*

THE 'IT' IN 'SH*T'

> *"Virtual meetings never work unless the tech is brilliant. And it never is"*

With its malevolent air duct tentacles, coffee machines dumping foul brown liquid onto the toast and botched plastic surgery operations, Terry Gilliam's 1985 film 'Brazil' highlights the dystopian chasm between what tech promises and what it can fail to deliver. And the dangerous consequences of over-reliance: that we become vulnerable to unjust outcomes from the most banal of automotive glitches. Computer says 'No!'

> "Everyone in the room joined on their iPads so those joining remotely could see the faces of those in the room. It was great in principle, but we wasted 45 minutes trying to eliminate the echoes"

The tech makes all the difference to the success of a virtual or hybrid meeting. When it works well, you don't notice it - the meeting is enhanced and flows as it should; but when it doesn't, it's a squeaky wheel:

> "Dress shabbily and they remember the dress. Dress impeccably and they remember the woman"
>
> **- Coco Chanel**

When the tech goes wrong, it is incredibly frustrating. We feel powerless and it's all we can think about: dodgy WIFI causing pictures to freeze or sound to be delivered in packets, echoes, being on mute, microphones not working, not being able to see the Lowry stickmen sitting round the table. No one is paying attention to what is actually being said.

How are people managing their techstrations?

The smooth-running of the meeting is only as reliable as the weakest link in its IT chain. Whilst people's home set-ups are not controllable, a well-run board can take action to minimise IT pitfall pain. Simply having someone on stand-by throughout the meeting is a good place to start:

Investing in the best, state-of-the-art kit can work, although it may not necessarily be within budget. Cheaper practicalities like positioning multiple microphones down the middle of the table or hanging them from the ceiling can solve the problem of not being able to hear. A really big screen helps when there are a lot of people joining remotely, maximising the size and number of faces visible at any one time.

But sometimes the best kit doesn't quite live up to the hype.

To get round the issue of virtual joiners getting the matchstick men view, owl cameras whizz round to focus on the person who is speaking. This is effective if the sensitivity is right, but often they are either too slow to respond or too sensitive, spinning to the stirring of a coffee cup or the shuffling of papers.

7.4 OILING THE WHEELS

COMPANY SECRETARIAT

Really well-run boards have a dedicated company secretariat function, able to shift things around last minute and oversee the practicalities of running a board. The best-of-the-bunch ensure that purpose is clear, that papers are slick and appropriately detailed and trail upcoming regulations and issues that may impact the board. A great company secretariat is often under-appreciated, yet can be crucial to determining the board's effectiveness.

> *"Two of my boards are in-house. The papers are concise and they arrive on time in one cohesive pack of information. The other board uses an out-sourced co-sec. There is a massive problem with quality and timeliness. Papers are not well-collated and they are drip-fed. There is a big difference"*

Case Study: Report Writing Training

Communication is so key, particularly writing a paper that tells you what the issue is and how to address it. Report-writing for boards is pretty weak. Our co-sec runs training courses on how to get it right.

Some boards also have a board sherpa, distinct from the company secretary. Serving as a bridge between the board and the organisation, they provide a separate and dedicated secretariat function for the NEDs independent of the CEO's office and are particularly helpful for onboarding and orientating.

Case Study: What the Company Secretary Said

The company secretary should be seen and not heard: if I'm doing my job properly, I'm not needed at all in the meeting itself. And that's all down to the quality of the preparation and my closeness to the board, to the chair and to the presenters.

Good governance is about expediting decision-making, being really clear about who can make the decisions. It should not be about over-burdening people with red tape. It's always easier in smaller organisations where interpersonal relationships are good, but there's only so far that informal discussion can take you. Boards centralise the process. But the meetings have to be worthwhile. You need to invite the right people. A lot of people feel like they want to be in the room, until they are actually there.

A big part of my role is building trust via networking, holding informal internal meetings, anticipating what will be needed at future meetings. I sit outside the CEO's door and I have a really close relationship with the chair; I see my principal role as representing him when he's not in the room.

I'm responsible for the overall crafting of the agenda, deciding the running order and the time allocations. I try to do it thematically. In a two-to-three-hour meeting, the sweet spot is about 15 minutes in, so I schedule the more contentious matters up-front and park the governance stuff towards the end.

Board Papers are a constant battle and I have four ground rules: keep it brief, no acronyms, summarise previous on-topic discussions and write as if you are explaining something to your mum. I require a consistent format (we have a three-page guideline document), which we reinforce via training. We get the 40 people who regularly write board papers in a room together and then the chair and two Ned's talk about what they need from a paper. The team is reminded that they are part of a whole and that their paper is one of many that the board has to consider.

A month before the board meeting, I meet with the executive responsible for producing the paper and discuss its thrust, format, who else to speak to for input and when I'll need it for review. If there are real problems with a paper, I will rewrite it, but that's only happened once or twice. And it really shouldn't happen at all because of all the pre-work.

I also oversee training for board directors. I run a standard one-and-a-half hour induction programme for new directors and ongoing training too, typically covering topical items. These sessions are not minuted and we invite subject matter experts. They tend to be relatively junior, which has the added benefit of directors broadening their reach and getting a deeper flavour of the organisation.

So basically I'm responsible for the smooth-running of the meetings. And I'm a control-freak. But I have to be: I need to think about every aspect, from the timing of the coffee breaks, to the temperature of the room, to making sure there are fully-charged power packs on hand in case people's kit runs out of juice. And I live and learn: one time we left the window open, and a pigeon flew into the boardroom. I won't be doing that again.

SOCIAL CHAIR

WTW's The Thinking Ahead Institute's 2018 thought piece on Better Decision Making[11] researched methods of running meetings more effectively, setting out typical pitfalls and potential solutions. They suggest appointing a social chair.

Whilst not participating in the meeting themselves, the social chair's role is to ensure that everyone else is involved: everyone should have a voice, no one should be allowed to dominate the discussion and seniors should speak last. And ensuring the discussion is constructive, asking critics for alternative suggestions as opposed to simply shouting down ideas.

Even though this function is currently carried out by the chair on most boards, it might be a useful addition particularly in virtual and hybrid meetings, to allow the chair to focus more on the discussion and the decision-making.

---

[11] Better Decision-making: A Tool Kit - Thinking Ahead Institute, Willis Towers Watson (2018)

FORMALITY

> *"Boards shouldn't be too dry - they shouldn't lack life.
> I like a bit of humour and fun, some
> camaraderie and collaboration"*

Board meetings can be a bit formal, and rightly so, given the associated risks and the seriousness of the decisions. However, creating space and giving permission for fun and creativity can be helpful. Playfulness can be good, generating a constructive and energising atmosphere for innovation.

ROUND TABLES

Board members' decisions carry equal weight and they should be encouraged to contribute equally. The shape of the boardroom table can have a profound effect on this. King Arthur was an egalitarian! He sat his knights around a round table for a reason, demonstrating that they were all of equal importance and stature.

To encourage equal participation in a meeting, round tables work the best. Oval tables are better than rectangular.

THE FOUR-HOUR PLUS MEETING

Schools structure lessons into 40-minute blocks to retain their students' attention spans. Health and Safety guidelines suggest that we should have regular short breaks. And frequent headline-grabbers claim that our average attention span is shorter than a goldfish's, whilst others point out that it is long enough for us to devour an entire series of "Breaking Bad" in one sitting. Clearly the answer sits somewhere in between and is a function of how engaged we are in the subject matter.

Are board meetings too long?

Time Waits For No Man

Board meetings have evolved into their current shape and rhythm for a reason. Often driven by the quarterly reporting cycle, there is a set amount of material that needs to be got through and together these determine the minimum length and frequency.

Couple this with the practicalities of getting senior folk together for the board meeting. Busy people with busy diaries, having to travel. It makes perfect sense - from a logistical point of view at least - to have as few meetings as possible and to pack as much into each of them as the day allows. But does it make perfect sense from a cognitive perspective? You need to factor in regular breaks for people's brains to function. And some meetings run for six or more hours.

"Board meetings are all about the catering. Keep people comfortable"

Given the new freedoms in our post-pandemic world, would it make sense to challenge the traditional quarterly board meeting cycle?

Could a four-hour quarterly board meeting sensibly morph into one two-hour meeting after quarter end, with two follow-up one-hour long monthly virtual meetings?

EMAIL ACCESS

Accessing emails can be problematic for NEDs if their organisation has very tight security. Is there a better way?

Case Study: Email Access

IT security can be horrendous for people who are not full-time employees. I can't access my board-related emails on my personal phone. It is so inefficient - security and confidentiality are obviously really important, but there needs to be some adaptation to allow for the way NEDs operate.

Hidden Secrets

8. OTHER THOUGHTS

8.1 SUMMARY

1. Engaging with employees and factoring in their unfiltered views in boardroom discussions is part of a director's role. Ways to achieve this include setting up an Employee Consultation Group that reports periodically to the board and to have a director with designated responsibility for it

2. Over-boarding can cause conflicts and workload problems. There are regulatory and investor-imposed limits to the number of roles a director can take on

3. Levels of directors' remuneration may be a contributing factor in the propensity to over-board

4. Arguments against increasing directors' remuneration include compromising the director's ability to walk away from a position. Arguments in favour include the diversity benefits of making board roles accessible to less financially-secure candidates

5. The "you have to have one to get one" requirement of many hiring boards makes it difficult for first time NEDs to secure an appointment. Perseverance pays off!

8.2 EMPLOYEE ENGAGEMENT

Part of the role of the board director is to engage with the employees of the business. In the UK, this is formalised as a governance requirement for the board to consider the views of employees via a route independent of the exec.

> "Social media has made it even more important to be clear and consistent in employee engagement and how to communicate the ethos. Be clear about what you are trying to do and be unambiguous in how you do it or people will fill in the blanks themselves. Be authentic. They don't have to like you. They just have to be clear about who you are and what you stand for"

It can be very difficult to engage with employees and there is no one-size-fits-all. Some firms have active, vibrant forums, some have effective internal newsletters, intranets and chat facilities. Some use surveys which can generate interesting output, although preserving anonymity often makes it hard to identify specific needs. And there is ongoing debate about their effectiveness with survey fatigue and the Uncertainty Principle effect: whether the act of taking the survey affects the behaviours it is trying to observe and measure.

The complexities around working patterns mean it is no longer simply a case of directors walking the floors once a quarter or chatting to someone on a factory production line. People work part-time and have zero hours contracts; with hybrid policies, people are often at home, with some working fully-remotely. So what is the solution?

One approach is for the business to establish an 'Employee Consultation Group' that reports formally to the board every quarter. The rhythm and systematisation gives credibility by demonstrating it is not a one-off gimmick produced especially for the board.

Another is to designate a board member with responsibility for employee engagement. With the help of HR, they can dip into different conversations, liaise with trade unions and report back. This model is helpful if executed well, but comes under strain if the business is located in multiple countries.

Case Study: Employee Engagement

Our board goes to different locations to attend town halls. Whilst not sufficient, it is really useful to get a handle on what is going on. You get "A-ha!" moments from listening to the questions.

"If someone on the board has responsibility for employee engagement, they will think creatively about how best to do it"

8.3 OVER-BOARDING

Over-boarding - when a director takes on so many board seats that they are unable to devote sufficient time and focus to fulfil their duties - has been a topic of debate for years. Whilst the upper limits are not always crystal-clear, guidance has come via formalised corporate governance codes, interwoven with investors' quest for good stewardship.

Many large institutional investors and asset managers now have defined and publicly-stated policies, stating how many other positions an individual can hold if they are a) a CEO of a public company, b) an executive of a public company and c) a NED; these limits determine their approach to proxy voting and sometimes whether they will invest in, or continue to hold, a company's shares.

Whilst guidelines are helpful, they are only ever that. Some boards take up more time than others and some individual directors are more adept at juggling.

> *"One of our NEDs is over-boarding. She's very good, but there is always a crisis on one of her boards and it becomes very difficult to focus if two crises happen at once"*

In an ideal world, over-boarding would be self-regulated. NEDs want to do a good job, after all. However, as people actively choose to leave executive life earlier in their careers to pursue a portfolio of roles, being a professional NED has become commonplace and with it the desire, and need, to earn money. This can lead to NEDs accumulating board positions.

8.4 DIRECTORS' REMUNERATION

Are NEDs paid enough, given the responsibilities and risks they take on as a director?

> *"There is lots of groaning that the risks of being a director have increased disproportionately given the fees. But the risks are very small if directors and boards are doing their job properly"*

The advertised days for a NED role typically understate the time required. And this is just to deal with the everyday business; a crisis can take up an enormous amount of non-executive time. Yet NEDs are paid a fraction compared with their executive counterparts.

There is a strong argument for **not** increasing NEDs' pay:

> *"As a NED, you have to be able to walk away, otherwise you compromise your independence. I struggle with younger people having portfolio careers, as they can't walk away when they are reliant on the income. And so I don't think it's a great idea to bump up NED remuneration as then it becomes a job"*

However, whilst compelling, this leads to a fundamental problem. Taking the argument to its logical conclusion means that the only people who could take on a NED role are those who don't need the money. In practice, this results in a skew toward rich people and/or pensioners, significantly limiting the diversity of candidates.

> *"As Chris Rock said: you don't need segregation, it's called 'The Price'. If you have unpaid directors, you narrow the pool to people with no money problems. Or retired people"*

Perhaps NEDs become even more invested when they are paid well. And the more they are paid, the fewer they will need and the risk of over-boarding diminishes.

8.5 SECURING THAT ELUSIVE FIRST NED

> *"You have to have one to get one"*

It can take a long time to get your first NED appointment. For many of my reference group, we are talking years rather than months, with countless rounds of time-consuming applications, interviews and rejections. A commonly-cited rebuttal is that Catch 22 of needing to have board experience before you can be appointed.

Whilst some boards are honest about this up-front, others are not and say they will consider first time NEDs. But often when it comes to the crunch, boards play safe and take experience over enthusiasm and fresh ideas in their concern that a new NED will not understand where the non-executive role ends and the executive role starts. So, the upshot is that you have to be significantly better than your experienced rivals to stand a chance of being appointed.

And so boards keep recycling the same old candidates, and the pool of appointable NEDs risks becomes stale.

This flies in the face of diversity.

This can be deeply frustrating for aspiring NEDs. The unanimous advice is to keep kissing the frogs. Eventually, you will encounter the prince who recognises that your unique skills outweigh any perceived risks. Then other appointments will quickly follow and you will be on your way.

Rainbow Connection

Copyright © 2023 Jenny Segal

9. IN CONCLUSION

An effective board arises from effective individuals interacting effectively. Whilst there is some mysticism around creating the magic of the group dynamic, a lot of it boils down to having great NEDs who are engaged and really care, under the guidance of a fantastic chair.

Being a NED is ever-more challenging as business become more complex, new threats and opportunities emerge and the regulator keeps an increasingly-interested eye. You can't just do it to collect the fees and for the pinnacle-of-your-career badge. You need to be good at it. And, as with all things motivation-related, that generally means you need to enjoy it. Which means you need to be shouting 'YES!!' when you ask yourself these three questions:

1. **Does the business interest me?**
2. **Can I add value?**
3. **Do I like the other members of the board?**

And you need to start with at least a 9 out of 10 for each of them, otherwise your enthusiasm **will** wane over time.

I hope you found this collection of wisdom a handy guide for how to make bad boards better and good boards great. And that it provides insightful guidance for aspiring and new NEDs, whilst serving as a useful touchstone for those with a wealth of experience.

Brave and Beautiful

INDEX

A

abundance mentality, 77
agenda, 24, 32, 40, 44, 45, 49, 50, 51, 60, 62, 67, 99, 108
alchemy, 56, 58
Apprentice, The, 17

B

black swans, 51
board dinners, 21, 62, 63, 64
board sherpa, 115
Brazil, 113
Breaking Bad, 118
Bridgeland, Sally, ii, ix, 79, 80

C

chemistry, 22, 24, 30, 53, 56, 58, 59, 66, 67
chess club - drama club, 79, 80, 97
coach, 67
committee chairs, 30
company secretariat, 24, 30, 32, 92, 96, 102, 105
company secretary, 110, 112, 115
conductor, 40, 41
conflicts of interest, 37
CPD, 53, 67
cream, 74
culture, i, ii, 17, 26, 32, 46, 47, 48, 53, 55, 56, 63, 67, 74

D

diversity
cognitive, 54, 75, 77, 78, 81
international, 78
visible, 75
Douglas Adams, 94
dysfunction, 36
dyslexia, 80

E

Effectiveness Barometer, 26
effectiveness reviews, 25
ethnic minority, 76

F

field trips, 64

G

Goldilocks, 101
governance, 33, 35, 37, 88, 123, 124
gray rhinos, 51
groupthink, 57, 75, 76, 82

H

Harvard Business Review, 83, 84
Hemingway, Ernest, 100
Hitch-hiker's Guide to the Galaxy, The, 94
hobby horses, 27

I

imposter syndrome, 77

J

jam, 74
jargon, 101

K

King Arthur, 118

M

Martin, Tim, 87
Monty Python, 17
motivation, i, 129

O

onion, 98
over-boarding, 124

P

portals, 91, 92
pro bono, 46
protocols, 60, 110, 112
purpose, 24, 29, 30, 33, 62, 76, 85, 87, 91, 99, 105

Q

quotas, 76

R

references, vii, 70, 73
reflection time, 24, 50
Reginald Perrin, 17
regulator, 33, 36, 60, 64, 91, 95, 129
remuneration, 69, 125, 126
respect, 24, 30
Rock, Chris, 126
round table, 43, 118

S

shareholder, 37
skills, 22, 24, 29, 40, 54, 55, 56, 57, 67, 69, 70, 71, 73, 76, 77, 108
social chair, 105, 117
social signalling, 54, 76
stakeholder, viii, 30, 36, 37, 59, 61, 65, 76, 85, 86
strategy days, 65, 67
strengths, 22, 46, 54, 56, 73, 74, 100
subsidiary, 33, 88
Succession, 17
Sugar, Lord Alan, 17
surveys, 123

T

techstraction, 111
techstration, 113
Thinking Ahead Institute, 117
timeliness, 56, 91, 102, 115
training, 53, 64, 65, 66, 115

V

vulnerable, 55, 113

Stairway To Wisdom